Cutting Edge in Science

Shuhoh Matsuno
Ruskyle L. Howser

KINSEIDO

Kinseido Publishing Co., Ltd.
3-21 Kanda Jimbo-cho, Chiyoda-ku,
Tokyo 101-0051, Japan

Copyright © 2005 by Shuhoh Matsuno
　　　　　　　　　Ruskyle L. Howser

All rights reserved. No part of this publication may be reproduced, stored in a retrieval system, or transmitted, in any form or by any means, electronic, mechanical, photocopying, recording or otherwise, without the prior permission of Kinseido Publishing Co., Ltd.

First published 2005 by Kinseido Publishing Co., Ltd.

写真提供
P. 8, 24, 25, 40, 41, 56, 57, 72, 73,
US Dept. of Agriculture—Agricultural Reserch Service
Pacific Northwest National Laboratory
Sandia National Laboratory
Oak Ridge National Laboratory
National Laboratory
National Cancer Institute—Visual Online
US Dept. of Defense—Defense Link News Photos

イラスト
佐藤衿子

はじめに

　「科学学習」を楽しみ，「有益情報」を手に入れ，「理系マインド」を育て，おまけに「英語力アップ」も実現するテキスト。こんな大それたコンセプトを視野に入れ，書き下ろしたのが本書です。理系だけでなく文系の学生諸君にも，「聴いて納得，読んでためになる」，そしてさらに「実践力が身に付く」テキスト作りを心がけました。

　特に，将来の就職を大きく左右する，「TOEICテスト対策」を意識し，「リスニング」に重点をおいたことが本テキストの一大特色といえます。本テキストのエクササイズを通し，希望する就職先が一歩も二歩も身近になることでしょう。

　ここで本テキストの特色を列記してみると，

① 「科学情報アクセス」と「TOEICテスト対策」が同時にできる。
② 各章のトピックは，最新の話題性のあるものにしぼり，しかも，リスニング／リーディング／練習問題に一貫性を持たせ，相乗効果 (synergy) による効果的な学習ができる。
③ 毎章，リスニングでは，TOEICのパート別特徴を把握し，かつ得点アップの具体策を *Check it out!* でたてられる。
④ リーディングでは，内容に関する英問英答にとどまらず，TOEICリーディング対策を意識し，空所補充問題・誤文指摘問題が配備されている。
⑤ 本書の活きた最新の情報記事や *For Your Information* は，学際的知識として役立つだけでなく，日常会話の話題としても興味深い内容となっている。

　本テキストで学習することを契機とし，インターネット，新聞，雑誌などを活用し，幅広い分野に目を向けていただければと思います。そのためのツールとして，英語スキルを高めることは大きな意味を持ってきます。ネットなどによる英語情報へのアクセスとその読み取りは，我々の間に明らかな「情報格差」(information divide) を生んでいます。IT時代を生きる皆さんには，そのことを踏まえて英語を学習し，使えるようになっていただきたいと思います。

　最後に，科学学習のパートナーとして最適のサイトを1つ紹介しておきましょう。

http://www.earthsky.com

　バラエティに富む短めの記事を目で確認できるのみならず，音声も聞けるので大変役に立ちます。毎日更新される，このサイトを追っかけてみて下さい。英語マインドが改善され，理系マインドも育つことうけあいです。

Great works are preformed, not by strength, but perseverance.
　　　　　　　　　　　　　　　　——*Samuel Johnson*
「偉大な作品とは，腕力ではなく，忍耐の結晶である」
　　　　　　　　　　　　　　　　サミュエル・ジョンソン

2002年9月吉日
松野　守峰
Ruskyle L. Howser

本書の使い方

PART 1 SCIENCE TOPICS

VOCABULARY　簡単なボキャブラリーのチェックをします。あらかじめリスニングに出てくる単語をいくつか知ることができますので，スムーズに次のアクティビティに移行できます。

LISTENING　実践的なコミュニケーション能力を測る目安になる，TOEIC形式でのリスニングをおこなうセクションです。サイエンスに関する情報の聴き取りがメインですが，英語の仕掛けは限りなく実際のTOEICに近づけてあります。以下に簡単に，TOEICのリスニング問題形式を紹介しておきましょう。

　　PartⅠ：写真描写問題：写真を見て，放送される4つの英文を聴き，最も写真の描写として適切なものを選ぶ問題
　　PartⅡ：応答問題：英語での問いかけに対し，続いて放送される3つの英文を聴いて，最も適切な応答文を選ぶ問題
　　PartⅢ：会話問題：X→Y→X の会話を聴いて，その内容に関する質問に答える問題。
　　PartⅣ：説明文問題：音声案内，コマーシャル，ニュース，スピーチなどを聴き取り，質問に答える問題

この4つのパートを各課のリスニングで順番に学習することで，総合的なリスニング力を養成します。最初の4課までは一通り問題形式に慣れるために，英文スクリプトを表記してあります。また，付属のカセットテープは，スロースピードとナチュラルスピードの2種類を用意しました。学習者のレベルに応じてご使用いただけます。

Check it out !　TOEICのスコアを上げるための対策を，ポイントを絞って解説するコラムです。試験であわてないための心構えから具体的な対策，英語学習の方法まで，得点アップのコツを取り上げました。

READING　サイエンスに関する，まとまった内容の英文を読んだり，図やグラフを見て，4つの英語の質問に答えていくセクションです。最初の2題は，英文の読解ができたかを確かめる問題です。3題目と4題目はそれぞれ，空所補充問題と誤文指摘問題となっており，文法や語法の知識が問われます。これらはそれぞれ，TOEICのリーディング問題の形式に準拠したものです。

PART 2 RELATED ARTICLE

その課のトピックに関連した英語情報を盛り込んだ，バラエティーに富むエクササイズを設けました。日本語文や語句の解説をヒントにして設問に答える形式です。各課で扱っているトピックを違った角度から見ることができますので，学んだことが切り口をかえた立体的な知識として理解されます。

For Your Information　　サイエンストピックに関する，最新情報や参考になるデータなどを日本語で紹介します。興味のある素材が見つかったら，学習者はこれについて自分で調べてみると，さらに新事実が発見できるかもしれません。

TOEICについて

　TOEICは200問の問題を2時間で解く客観式テストです。Listening PartⅠ-Ⅳ（100問 / 45分）とReading PartⅤ-Ⅶ（100問 / 75分）のセクションから構成されています。このテストを開発したアメリカの試験公共機関 ETS (Educational Testing Service) は，TOEFL, SATなどの過去の膨大なデータを蓄積しており，それを基に聴く能力の約70％が話す能力を，読む能力の約60％が書く能力を反映するようにTOEICテストを作成しています。テスト中には，休憩がないため，かなりの集中力とスタミナが要求されます。受験する場合は，あらかじめ，よく問題形式に慣れておく必要があるでしょう。

Contents

1. Electronic Ink ·· 8
   ◆電子的インク

2. Botox ··· 12
   ◆ボトックス

3. Earthquake Prediction ··· 16
   ◆地震予知

4. Fuel Cells ·· 20
   ◆燃料電池

5. Traveling ··· 24
   ◆旅 行

6. Violence Gene ·· 28
   ◆暴力的遺伝子

7. Smart Buildings··· 32
   ◆ハイテクビル

8. Asteroid Busting ·· 36
   ◆小惑星爆発

9. Emerging Diseases ··· 40
   ◆新種の病気

10. Atlantic Heat Conveyor Currents ································· 44
    ◆大西洋暖流コンベヤー

11. *Unexceptional Beauty* ････････････････････････････ 48
    ◆絶世の美人

12. *Flight Simulators* ･････････････････････････････････ 52
    ◆模擬飛行訓練装置

13. *Return of the Mammoth* ･････････････････････････ 56
    ◆マンモスの再現

14. *Echelon* ･･ 60
    ◆エシュロン

15. *Spider Ranching* ･･････････････････････････････ 64
    ◆クモの牧場化

16. *Europa's Icy Sea* ･･････････････････････････････ 68
    ◆エウロペの氷の海

17. *Microbots* ･･････････････････････････････････････ 72
    ◆マイクロボット

18. *Alien Hitchhikers* ･･････････････････････････････ 76
    ◆宇宙からのヒッチハイカー

19. *Land Mines* ････････････････････････････････････ 80
    ◆地 雷

20. *Child Prodigy*･･････････････････････････････････ 84
    ◆神 童

1. Electronic Ink

電子的インク

PART 1 SCIENCE TOPICS

　紙が発明されたのは中国で紀元後105年頃。現在，世界中の紙の年間消費量は2億8000万トンで，Ａ4サイズ用紙に換算すると，なんと56兆枚にもなります。そしてみなさんも御承知の，世界で最も権威があるとされる英語の辞典「オックスフォード大英々辞典」フルセット20冊，この重さをこの間，計測してみました。どの位あったと思いますか？　150ポンドもありました。知性の重さには敬意を払いますが，パルプ材の消費も気になります。近年，官庁も企業も民間も，ペーパーレスの方向に動いているのは歓迎すべき事実でしょう。

VOCABULARY

▶ Write the English words that correspond to following Japanese words.

1. モニター→m _____
2. デザイン→d _____
3. ア　ポ　→ap _____
4. シリアル→c _____
5. キッチン→k _____

LISTENING

▶ Listen to the tape, and mark your answers.

Ex.

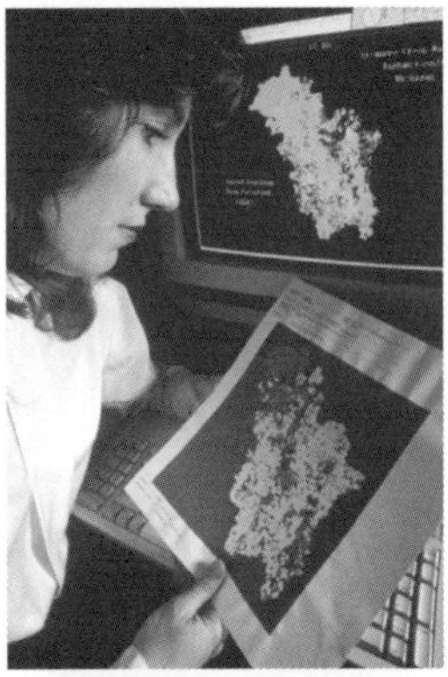

1.

2.

3.

4.

▶ **Fill in the circles that match your answers.**

Ex. (A) She is painting a picture from memory.
    (B) The prince has come to the castle to meet her.
    (C) The book on the desk is very thick and heavy.
    (D) The woman is looking at a print from the computer.   Ⓐ Ⓑ Ⓒ ●

1. (A) The two men are walking together in the park.
   (B) The computer has been boxed up for shipping.
   (C) One man is pointing at the computer monitor screen.
   (D) Nothing has been left on the table for him to work with.   Ⓐ Ⓑ Ⓒ Ⓓ

2. (A) The book is being viewed on a big screen.
   (B) The man is filling out a table with information.
   (C) He is drawing a design on the long, thin pages.
   (D) The book is being printed on a modern printing press.   Ⓐ Ⓑ Ⓒ Ⓓ

3. (A) The kitchen is deserted at this hour of the day.
   (B) She is eating a bowl of breakfast cereal.
   (C) She is putting something into the small round bowl.
   (D) The table is too high for her to reach anything on it.   Ⓐ Ⓑ Ⓒ Ⓓ

4. (A) This library offers only hardcover reference books.
   (B) She is reading in the room before her appointment.
   (C) The big flowers she is holding in her lap are beautiful.
   (D) The woman is taking notes about her work on the farm.   Ⓐ Ⓑ Ⓒ Ⓓ

── *Check it out !* ──

　TOEIC®テストを受けると，最初に取り組むのが「リスニング」で，45分を使い100問に答えていきます。Part Ⅰ / Part Ⅱ / Part Ⅲ / Part Ⅳ の4部構成で，トップバッターが「写真描写問題」（Pictures）の20問。放送で流れる音声スピードは200語／分で，英語のネイティブ・スピードに慣れていない耳には「ハヤイ・ヤバイ」と感じられるはず。でも，ご安心を！　このコーナーでは，毎回TOEIC®のリスニングのコツを紹介していきます。よく身につけてスコアアップにつなげましょう。

Electronic Ink

READING

▶ Read the following passage and answer the questions after it. Questions #1 and #2 test your comprehension. In Question #3, choose the answer that best completes the sentence. In Question #4, find the error in the sentence.

Programmable Paper

Paper is cheap and easier to read than a computer screen, but it is difficult to use it more than once. Two companies are trying to change that. They are developing electronic ink displays. Painted on a thin sheet of plastic, they will look and feel like paper. But unlike paper, they will be programmable. With small, powerful data storage devices, electronic ink books will hold huge amounts of information.

Both companies' products work on the same principle. Electrically charged black chips float in tiny, oil-filled pockets. By applying an electrical charge to the pocket, the chips are either pulled to the surface or the bottom. In a grid, the pockets work like the pixels on your computer screen, making the text from tiny black and white dots. New texts can be downloaded from a computer or the Internet. Electronic ink displays will look and feel like a book, but have all the functions and flexibility of a computer.

1. In what ways is old-fashioned paper superior to an LCD screen?
    (A) It is heavier.
    (B) It is breakable.
    (C) It is easier to read.
    (D) It is programmable.

2. How is an electronic ink book better than a regular book?
    (A) It holds more data in a small size.
    (B) It is cheaper than a regular paper book.
    (C) It is able to sell many different texts.
    (D) It is bigger than an equal size English dictionary.

3. The paper book will probably become a _____ as publishing goes electronic.
    (A) antique (B) novelty (C) unusual (D) rare

4. <u>Many</u> historically famous science <u>text</u> are now <u>available</u> on the Internet.
     (A)   (B)   (C) (D)

PART 2 RELATED ARTICLE

米欧英の新学期の最初の授業は，どのような幕あけをするのかちょっと授業の風景をのぞいてみることにしましょう。「大体こんな具合にスタートするのか」と英語で押さえておくと，違和感なく良いスタートを切れるでしょう。英語に相当する日本語を空所に入れてみてください。

Initial Icebreaker For The New Academic Year

Good morning, everyone. My name is Professor Franklin Winston. This is Engineering 143, Introduction To Materials Science. We'll be looking at the basic properties of most common structural materials in the coming academic year. First term, we'll focus on naturally occurring materials, and during the second term we'll take a look at the future of synthetic materials. You won't be surprised to hear that there will be a final at the end of each term. As for attendance, 80 percent is required to pass my class and I'll be checking. There will be periodic assignments, and all homework must be emailed to my Web site by the due date. Are there any questions?

諸君，おはよう！私は教授のフランクリン・ウィンストンです。このクラスは工業科143の「資材科学入門」です。これから1年かけて，最もよく知られている建築資材の基本的（　　　　）について学習していきます。（　　　　）では，自然発生の材料を（　　　　）授業は展開し，後期は，（　　　　）資材の展望に焦点を当てて授業は進むことになりますので，そのつもりでいて下さい。なお，出席率に関しては，私のクラスの場合，8割がミニマムになります。しかも，出欠は毎回取ります。また，宿題は定期的にあり，全ての宿題は締切日までに私のホームページに（　　　　）して下さい。質問はあるかな？

【語句】initial icebreaker「開講のコトバ」，You won't be surprised to hear ～「皆さんは～ということを聞いても別段おどろかれることはないでしょう」，As for attendance「出席率に関していうと」，I'll be checking (whether or not you are present) <省略に注意>「毎回，出欠をチェックする」，periodic assignments「定期的に出される宿題」，by the due date「期日までに」

For Your Information

「電子的インク」技術の開発にちからを入れているのが Xerox 社と E Ink 社。実用化には，ディスプレーに表示される文字をもっと読み易くする必要がある。Softbook 社・Rocket eBook 社では既に，電子的インク技術を利用した商品を販売しているが売れ行きはそれほど良くない。E Ink 社では，なんと図書館の書籍を丸ごと全部，持ち歩ける電子的インク本「1冊」に収納できる技術を開発中だ。近い将来，同技術を利用した表示を，スーパー・空港・株式市場の案内・広告・掲示で見かけるようになるだろう。LCD（液晶ディスプレー）より，50～100倍も節電できる電子的インクの技術は，やがて，新聞配達のサービスを恐竜と同じ運命をたどらせることになると言えよう。

Electronic Ink

2. *Botox*

ボトックス

PART 1 SCIENCE TOPICS

マドンナやマライヤ・キャリーが，ボトックス®注射を顔にほどこし，若返りに成功したということもあり，日本でも最近ではお手軽なプチ美容整形が注目されています。1989年，斜視（strabismus）・眼瞼痙攣（がんけんけいれん：blepharospasm）の治療薬としてボトックスは米食品医薬品局（the Food and Drug Administration: the FDA）の認可をうけました。ところが，ＦＤＡの認可がおりて以来，ボトックスは他の利用目的で世間に注目され，マスコミの関心を集めるようになったのです。

VOCABULARY

▶ Match the items in the two columns.

1. facelift
2. downtown
3. removal
4. injection
5. skin

a. main business area of a city
b. getting rid of something
c. administering a medicine with a syringe
d. the thin layer of tissue
e. cosmetic surgical operation

LISTENING

▶ Listen to the tape, and mark your answers.

Ex. "Good morning, John. How are you?"

   (A) "I am fine, thank you."
   (B) "I am in the living room."
   (C) "My name is John."

1. You are looking good. Have you lost weight?

   (A) Don't tell anyone, but I had a facelift.
   (B) No, I'm not going to tell you how much I weigh.
   (C) I'm just happy because I finally found what I was looking for.

2. I heard you went to the doctor yesterday. Are you OK?

   (A) Not at all. I'm feeling better than I've felt in years.
   (B) No problem. I just had a minor matter taken care of.
   (C) Yes, I've been feeling just awful the last couple weeks.

3. Don't you think you should start taking better care of yourself?

   (A) Yes, I'll take care of that right away, sir.
   (B) Sure, I think I'll start smoking cigarettes first.
   (C) You're probably right. I have been feeling a bit run down.

4. How do you stay so healthy and young looking?

   (A) It's just good genes, I guess.
   (B) No, I'm much older than most people think.
   (C) Without much exercise, I'm afraid you can't.

5. Which clinic do you recommend I go to for a procedure like that?

   (A) No, I think you should get a second opinion.
   (B) There are several well-known ones downtown.
   (C) That depends on whether you're hungry or not.

6. Who would you say is the best cosmetic surgeon in town?

   (A) I wouldn't know anything about that.
   (B) Yes, he's been in town a few months.
   (C) The doctor should be in tomorrow morning.

7. Are you sure laser surgery is safe to do on my eyes?

   (A) According to the statistcs it is a low-risk procedure.
   (B) Yes, I'm sure you will look much better with glasses.
   (C) I think it will be safer to leave it in the bank than at home.

— *Check it out!* —

　TOEIC®テストの「リスニング」で，2番目の課題として登場するのが，「応答問題」(Question-Response)の30問。「Part IIの問題指示文」は，約1分かけて音声放送で流されますから，この短い時間を利用し，3回大きく息をはき出し，深く息を吸いこむとよいでしょう。深呼吸は雑念を払い，集中力を高める効果があります。TOEIC®テストのすべてのパートの指示文は，毎回同じですから，あらかじめ頭に入れておきましょう。また，リスニング問題文はすべて「1度」しか読みあげられず，しかもPart IIだけは，正解の選択肢 Ⓐ Ⓑ Ⓒ も，放送音声だけを聴き答える「音声特化方式」です。つまり，問題文・選択肢ともに視覚によるヒントはなく，聴解力のみのパート，ということです。

READING

▶ Look at the following bar chart and answer the questions after it. Questions #1 and #2 test your comprehension. In Question #3, choose the answer that best completes the sentence. In Question #4, find the error in the sentence.

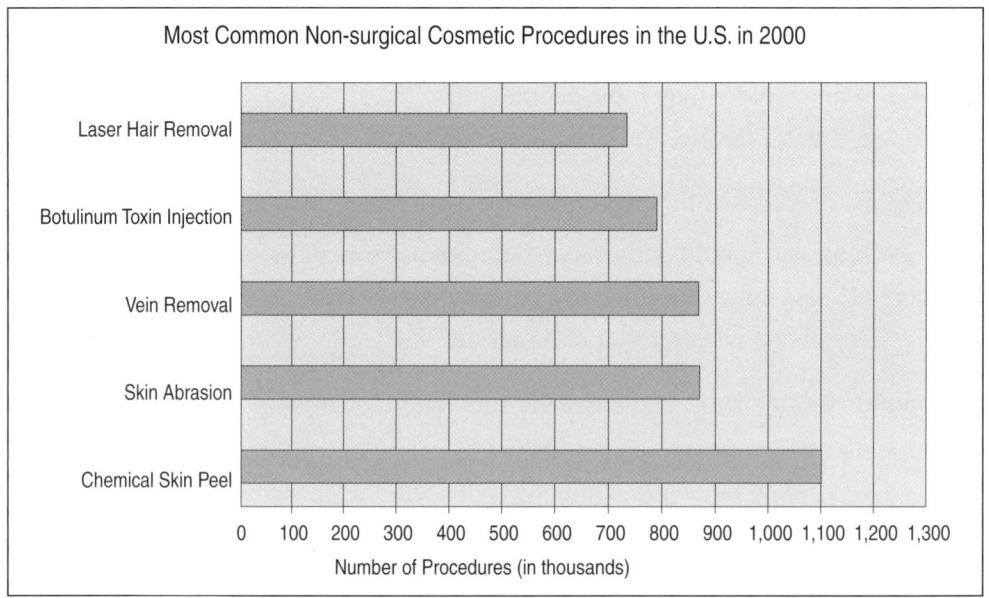

1. Which procedure was performed most often in the U.S. in the year 2000?

   (A) Skin abrasion.
   (B) Laser hair removal.
   (C) Chemical skin peel.
   (D) Botulinum toxin injection.

2. How many times were chemical skin peels done in 2000?

   (A) 100
   (B) 1,100
   (C) 1,300
   (D) 1,100,000

3. These reactions are _____ temporary, but can last several months.

   (A) generally   (B) general   (C) gentle   (D) genetic

4. The response is usually see 2-6 days after injection.
     (A)   (B) (C)   (D)

PART 2 RELATED ARTICLE

ボトックス関連の記事を英文で採りあげてみました。下に日本語訳をつけてありますから，これを参考にし，各空所をうめる適性な語を ⓐ〜ⓔ の中から１つずつ選んでみてください。

Botulinum Toxin Type A

Botox® is the brand name of botulinum toxin type A (¹   ) has been in use since about 1990. It is a protein (²   ) by the bacterium Clostridium botulinum. When (³   ) in medical settings as an injectable form of sterile, purified botulinum toxin, small doses of the toxin are injected (⁴   ) the affected muscles and block the release of the chemical acetylcholine that would otherwise signal the muscle to contract. The toxin thus paralyzes or weakens the (⁵   ) muscle.

ボトックスは，ボツリヌス菌タイプＡ型のブランド名のことで，1990年頃から利用されている。この菌は，「クロストリディアム・ボツリナム」と呼ばれるバクテリアが作り出す蛋白質のことである。減菌し，純化したボツリヌス菌を医療目的で注入する場合，少量の平常なら筋肉に収縮のシグナルを伝達する化学物質アセチルコリンの放出をストップさせる。その結果，ボツリヌス菌は注射した筋肉を麻痺（まひ）させたり，弱めたりすることになる。

ⓐ that ⓑ into ⓒ injected ⓓ used ⓔ produced

【語句】 be in use「利用される」, in medical settings「医療場面で」, sterile「滅菌した；殺菌した」, small doses of 〜「少量の〜」, the affected muscles「対象とする筋肉」, otherwise「ボツリヌス菌を注入しなければ」＜この単語は，コンテキストで訳を決めるしかない。たしかに辞書では，「別の方法で；他の点では；さもなければ」とあるが，掘り下げて内容をつかむことが必要。ここでは，otherwise = if the botulinum toxin is not injected, となる＞。

For Your Information

通常，ボトックスの効果は２〜６日で表れるが，どの位その効果が持続するかには個人差がある。普通は，３〜５ヶ月でもとに戻るが，４回・５回とボトックスの注射をくり返すと効用期間が長くなるといわれる。合衆国では，熟年男性役職者たちのボトックス利用が，2002年初期から急増している。なお，ボトックスによる典型的な副作用 (the most common adverse events) には，頭痛・呼吸器系感染 (respiratory infection)・流感に似た症状・眼瞼痙攣（がんけんけいれん：droopy eyelids）・吐き気 (nausea), がある。

3. Earthquake Prediction

地震予知

PART 1 SCIENCE TOPICS

地震予知研究の一環として，地震学者 (seismologists) は余震 (aftershock) と前震 (foreshock) のパターン研究に力を入れています。主な地震予知には，①Ｐ波変化 <地震の前に岩石の構成物質に変化が起きれば，地震波のスピードにも変化がおきるという仮説> ②地盤傾斜 (ground tilting) <断層 (fault) 沿いにゆがみ (stress) が蓄積すると，地盤に変化がおきる> ③ラドン・ガス上昇 <地震発生の前，周辺地域の深い井戸で，ラドン・ガス (radon gas) の放出量が上昇することが注目されている> ④導伝性変化 <地震発生周辺の岩石の導伝性 (electrical conductivity of rocks) が，地震の直前に変化することが観測されている>…などがあります。

VOCABULARY

▶ Choose the word that has the same meaning as the underlined one.

1. That's what we're trying to do with the current plan.
   a. directed   b. moved   c. being used now

2. Did you hear about the big quake last night?
   a. shaking of the ground   b. sudden violence   c. earth's crust

3. The plane is about to take off.
   a. is going to   b. has finished   c. is late

LISTENING

▶ Listen to the tape, and mark your answers.

1. A: Do we have emergency evacuation plans in case Mt. Rainier erupts?

   B: We made one a few years ago, but I don't know where it is.

   A: Let's find it and update it, just in case.

   What does the man recommend they do?

   (A) Evacuate the building immediately.

   (B) Find out the date of the next eruption.

   (C) Appoint someone to develop an emergency plan.

   (D) Make sure the plan is available and current.

   Ⓐ Ⓑ Ⓒ Ⓓ

2. A: Have we gotten the latest readings from the seismic sensors?

   B: They just came in a few minutes ago, but they don't show anything unusual happening.

   A: Even so, let's keep a close eye on them for the next few days.

   How much earthquake activity is currently happening?

   (A) Surprisingly little.

   (B) Much more than usual.

   (C) About the same amount as usual.

   (D) That information hasn't been received yet.   Ⓐ Ⓑ Ⓒ Ⓓ

3. A: Is your family in San Francisco OK?

   B: As far as I know. Why?

   A: Haven't you heard? They had a big earthquake this morning.

   Why isn't the woman worried about her family?

   (A) There are never any earthquakes in San Francisco.

   (B) She didn't know about the earthquake.

   (C) She hasn't heard where they live.

   (D) They live in a very safe house.   Ⓐ Ⓑ Ⓒ Ⓓ

4. A: What are these red areas on the map?

   B: Those are the areas of maximum danger in case of an earthquake.

   A: Really? It looks like we are right in the middle of one.

   What kind of information does the map show?

   (A) The frequency of earthquake tremors.

   (B) The locations of greatest risk in future earthquakes.

   (C) The places in which earthquakes have occurred most often.

   (D) The areas in which buildings are reinforced against earthquakes.   Ⓐ Ⓑ Ⓒ Ⓓ

― *Check it out !* ―

　TOEIC®テストの「リスニング」の３番手に登場するのが，Part Ⅲ「会話問題」（Short Conversations）で，出題数は30問。

　注意点は，Part Ⅰ / Part Ⅱと異なり「例題」は印刷されず，放送もされないことです。ただし，問題についての指示文と，指示文の音声放送はあります。他のパートと同様に，会話音声は１度しか流されません。会話の基本パターンは「X→Y→X」で，会話の構成は「女性と男性」「女性２人」「男性２人」です。

Earthquake Prediction

READING

▶ Read the following passage and answer the questions after it. Questions #1 and #2 test your comprehension. In Question #3, choose the answer that best completes the sentence. In Question #4, find the error in the sentence.

Quake Prediction

Ancient man told stories of gods and monsters to predict and explain earthquakes. Today, we understand more about the causes of quakes, but we still aren't much better at predicting when or where they will happen. The basics are clear. We live on giant plates of light stone that float on the surface of the earth, slowly moving around and crashing into each other. When the plates get stuck, the stress builds until they break loose. That is an earthquake. In theory, it should be simple to measure, but much of this is happening deep under the ground. So scientists have looked for the warning signals that an earthquake is about to happen. They have studied changes in electrical patterns or water levels in the earth, strange animal behavior and the patterns of small earthquakes that might indicate a big earthquake is coming. Scientists have been successful at more general predictions, but accurate, short-term predictions may be a long way off.

1. In the past, what did people think caused earthquakes?
    (A) Tectonic physics.
    (B) Electrical patterns.
    (C) Volcanic eruptions.
    (D) Supernatural creatures.

2. What is an earthquake?
    (A) The sudden movement of giant plates of stone.
    (B) The result of a change of underground water level.
    (C) A change in the rotation of the earth on its vertical axis.
    (D) A short-term prediction of how likely it is for a tsunami to occur.

3. Earthquakes can strike _____ warning and cause massive architectural damage.
    (A) before   (B) without   (C) until   (D) except

4. The Pacific Ocean is surrounded by a ring of seismic active regions.
               (A) (B)   (C)   (D)

PART 2 RELATED ARTICLE

合衆国のカリフォルニア州を縦断する形で，「サンアンドレアス断層」(San Andreas Fault)が走っていることはよく知られています。ここでは，1999年10月16日にカリフォルニア州をおそった，マグニチュード7.1の「ヘクター・マイン地震」(Hector Mine Earthquake)直後に出された，カリフォルニア緊急対策局 (the California Emergency Management Agency)の警報文を採りあげてみましょう。文意が整合性を持つように，ⓐ〜ⓓを並べかえてみて下さい。

ⓐ Basic emergency shelter equipment should also be kept on hand.
ⓑ And everyone is advised to make sure they have at least a three-day supply of fresh water and food, in addition to shelter.
ⓒ Further advisories will be issued as necessary.
ⓓ Residents should stay out of earthquake damaged buildings until inspectors have certified them as safe.

(   ) → (   ) → (   ) → (   )

【語句】emergency shelter equipment「緊急避難用道具」, be kept on hand「手元においておく」, a supply「備蓄」, advisories「情報」, be issued「出される」, as necessary「必要があれば」, stay out of 〜「〜に近づかない」, certify A as B「AをBと認定する」

For Your Information

1900年以降の世界中で発生した「強度別地震発生件数」を表にしてみました。

Frequency of Occurrence of Earthquakes Based on Observations since 1900

Descriptor（強度）	Magnitude（マグニチュード）	Average Annually（年間平均発生件数）
Great	8 and higher	1
Major	7 - 7.9	18
Strong	6 - 6.9	120
Moderate	5 - 5.9	800
Light	4 - 4.9	6,200 (estimated)
Minor	3 - 3.9	49,000 (estimated)
Very Minor	2 - 3	about 1,000 per day
	1 - 2	about 8,000 per day

Earthquake Prediction

4. Fuel Cells

燃料電池

PART 1 SCIENCE TOPICS

「燃料電池」とは，電気化学変換機器（electrochemical energy conversion device）のことで，水素と酸素を電気・熱に変換します。充電の必要のない燃料電池ですが，利用科学物質別により5〜6種のタイプがあります。燃料電池は直流（DC voltage）を供給し，モーター・明かり・家電製品の電源として利用可能で，利用科学物質しだいでは，発電所（power generation plants）・小型携帯電化製品・車の動力源としての応用が考えられます。そして，最も期待されているのがプロトン交換膜燃料電池（proton exchange membrane fuel cell: PEMFC）です。実用化の運びとなれば，車・バス・家庭の電力をすべてまかなえる「夢の電源」となるでしょう。

VOCABULARY

▶ Write the English words that correspond to following Japanese words.

1. 電力料金 → e_____ rates
2. 不足 → s_____
3. 干ばつ → d_____
4. ガソリン → g_____
5. ゴール → g_____

LISTENING

▶ Listen to the tape, and mark your answers.

Questions 1 through 3 refer to the following announcement.

> This is KDSL radio news. Our top story tonight is that electricity rates are going up again. At an emergency meeting Monday night, the state Energy Regulatory Commission approved an eight percent across-the-board increase. It is the fourth rate increase in the past eighteen months. The rise in rates is a direct result of the energy shortage in the western United States. Energy producers say the shortage has been caused in part by the drought that has left water reservoirs at record low levels. But critics claim that the energy companies are using the drought as an excuse to raise rates and drive up profits. Whatever the reason, wholesale energy rates have increased dramatically. The energy commission felt it had no choice but to pass along the increase to consumers. The increase will add about sixteen dollars to the monthly energy bill of the average family in the state.

1. Where would you hear this news?

    (A) On TV.
    (B) In a speech.
    (C) On the radio.
    (D) In a newspaper.

2. What is the main subject of this report?

    (A) The lack of rain.
    (B) The energy shortage.
    (C) The price of electricity.
    (D) The emergency commission.

3. Why do the energy utilities say prices are going up?

    (A) There hasn't been enough rain.
    (B) The number of consumers had increased.
    (C) Energy company profits haven't gone up.
    (D) The number of average families has decreased.

Check it out !

　TOEIC®テストの「リスニング」の最後に登場するのが，Part Ⅳ「説明文問題」(Short Talks) で，出題数は20問。注意点は，Part Ⅲ と同様，印刷された例題もなければ，例題放送もないことです。問題対象となる「課題」が，1度しか流れないのは他のパートと変わりがありませんが，他のパートに比べて長いので集中力が必要です。短いナレーションで約20秒，長いナレーションで約40秒，平均値をとると30秒になります。課題文の対象として採り上げられるのは，「公共アナウンス・録音音声案内・スピーチ・ニュース・社会一般」といった内容で，1つの課題放送について，2問～4問の「関連設問」がテストブックに印刷されています。最近の傾向としては，関連設問が2問型，あるいは3問型が主流といえるでしょう。

READING

▶ Read the following passage and answer the questions after it. Questions #1 and #2 test your comprehension. In Question #3, choose the answer that best completes the sentence. In Question #4, find the error in the sentence.

Future Electricity

Imagine if we had a cheap, clean, quiet way to make all the electricity we needed, anytime and anywhere. We wouldn't need any more gasoline for cars. We wouldn't need nuclear power plants or hydroelectric dams. Every house could have its own power plant. That has been the goal of engineers working on developing fuel cells, and it may not be that far away. Fuel cells convert hydrogen (H) and oxygen (O) into electricity, heat and water (H20). They capture the electrons that are released when water is made. It is very efficient. Fuel cells are already available. NASA has used them in its rockets and space shuttles for many years. But they are still too big and expensive to be practical for your home. Engineers are working to reduce both the cost and the size. Eventually, they expect to be able to use fuel cells to generate electricity not only in homes and cars, but even in cellphones and laptop computers.

1. How is a fuel cell different from a gasoline engine?
   (A) It uses the expansion of hot gases to generate power.
   (B) It runs on a much more dangerous and expensive fuel.
   (C) Electrical energy is captured directly from the chemical process.
   (D) It eliminates the loss of energy during long distance transmission.　Ⓐ Ⓑ Ⓒ Ⓓ

2. Where have fuel cells been effectively used for many years?
   (A) Computers.
   (B) Spaceships.
   (C) Gasoline engines.
   (D) Large power plants.　Ⓐ Ⓑ Ⓒ Ⓓ

3. Different engineering environments often call for _____ industrial designs.
   (A) different　(B) another　(C) otherwise　(D) the other　Ⓐ Ⓑ Ⓒ Ⓓ

4. The world economy simply cannot rely on energy made by fossil fuels forever.
   　　　　　　　　　　(A)　　　　　(B)　　　　　　　　(C)　　　　　　(D)
   　　　　　　　　　　　　　　　　　　　　　　　　　　　　　　　　Ⓐ Ⓑ Ⓒ Ⓓ

PART 2 RELATED ARTICLE

electricity「電気」の語源は，ギリシャ語の 'ēlektron'「琥珀（こはく）」で，コハクをこすると静電気現象 (electrostatic phenomena) が起こることによります。それでは，下に民間団体が雑誌に打った「節電広告文」をのせてみます。「発音記号表記」の部分を，「普通文字」に変換してみて下さい。

<例>　kæt → cat

(^{1}　taiəd　) of big electricity (^{2}　bilz　)? At Natural Energy Associates, we (^{3}　speʃəlaiz　) in designing and building energy (^{4}independənt) homes. Our homes get their (^{5}　pauər　) from safe, natural sources. We combine efficient design with (^{6}　soulər　) electric panels and wood burning stoves to (^{7}　iliməneit　) the need for outside electrical sources. You can save money and protect the environment by using only (^{8}　riju:zəbl　) energy. Call Natural Energy Associates today for a free estimate.

① 　　　　　　② 　　　　　　③
④ 　　　　　　⑤ 　　　　　　⑥
⑦ 　　　　　　⑧

【語句】combine A with B「AとBを合体させる」, efficient「効率を工夫した」, electric panels「パネルヒーター」, outside electrical sources「外部電源」, for a free estimate「無料の見積もりをうけるには」

For Your Information

　燃料電池の最大の阻害要因は，「水素」をどのようにして得るかにある。「酸素」は空気から採り入れればよいので簡単で，PEMFC方式の場合だと，カソード（電解槽：cathode）にポンプ採取すればよい。問題は水素の採り込み作業で，自宅に水素管を水素供給源からお手軽に引っぱりこんだり，ガソリンスタンド (gas station) に水素ポンプを常設し車に簡単に水素を入れることは，現時点では無理がある。水素は備蓄・供給がむずかしく，またインフラコストが非常に高くつくため，利用者負担が割高になる。結局，燃料電池の将来は，簡単便利な「燃料」を見つけ出せるかどうかにかかっている。

Fuel Cells

5. Traveling

旅 行

PART 1 SCIENCE TOPICS

新学期がスタートしてはや１ヶ月，気のはやい学生諸君の中には，もう夏のアルバイトと旅行計画を検討しているグループがちらほらいるようです。ここで，海外旅行関連のデータを紹介してみましょう。

▶ 2000年度の全世界の海外旅行者数は６億9880万人，売上高4758億ドル
▶ 2000年度の大陸別海外旅行者の獲得数１位はヨーロッパで，全世界の海外旅行者総数の57.7％を占め，4億330万人の海外旅行者数
▶ 2000年度に合衆国を訪れた海外旅行者の出費総額は１999年度比13.7％増の852億ドル
▶ 2000年度の米国人海外旅行者総数は6080万人で，旅行先のトップはメキシコの1880万人
▶ 2001年度の，米国内のネットを使った旅行チケット販売総額は２40億ドル。

VOCABULARY

▶ Match the items in the two columns.

1. field   ·   · a. an area of open land
2. hangar   ·   · b. a building for housing aircraft
3. current   ·   · c. a movable set of steps
4. crop   ·   · d. a body of water
5. ramp   ·   · e. a plant for food or other use

LISTENING

▶ Listen to the tape, and mark your answers.

1.

Ⓐ Ⓑ Ⓒ Ⓓ

2.

Ⓐ Ⓑ Ⓒ Ⓓ

3.

Ⓐ Ⓑ Ⓒ Ⓓ

4.

Ⓐ Ⓑ Ⓒ Ⓓ

5.

Ⓐ Ⓑ Ⓒ Ⓓ

6.

Ⓐ Ⓑ Ⓒ Ⓓ

― *Check it out !* ―

　テストブック中に印刷されている写真は「人物」が過半数を占め，しかも，「人物1人」の写真が圧倒的に多いと理解しておきましょう。ごくありふれた日常生活・オフィス内・作業現場などを扱った写真がメインです。Part Ⅰのリスニングのポイントはリスニング・セクションの導入部 <In this section of the test, you will have the chance to show how well you understand spoken English. There are four parts to this section, with special directions for each part.> と，このすぐ後に続く問題指示文が音声で流れる1分30秒を使って，深呼吸し集中力を高め出遅れないようにすることです。また，写真は，「人物／物の配置・位置関係・人物の動作」に，特に注意しましょう。

Traveling　25

READING

▶ Look at the following chart and answer the questions after it. Questions #1 and #2 test your comprehension. In Question#3, choose the answer that best completes the sentence. In Question #4, find the error in the sentence.

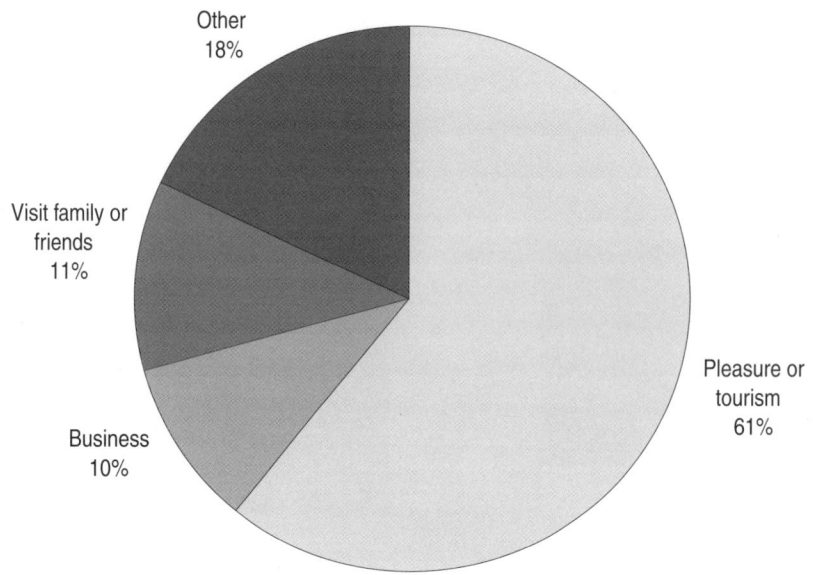

Reasons for travel by Canadians to America

1. What percentage of visits to America were not for business?
   (A) 10%   (B) 39%   (C) 61%   (D) 90%

2. How could the results of this survey best be summarized?
   (A) More than half of all Canadian visitors did not come to America at all.
   (B) The majority of visitors to the United States came for business purposes.
   (C) Most Canadians visit America just to enjoy themselves and see the country.
   (D) Most people who answered were not willing to state their reasons for traveling.

3. Tourists sometimes have a negative _____ on the cultures of the places they visit.
   (A) impact   (B) troubling   (C) destruction   (D) ecological

4. International air travel has boomed as a result to the decline in average fare prices.
                                   (A)   (B)   (C)   (D)

PART 2 RELATED ARTICLE

2001年9月11日に合衆国で発生した「同時多発テロ」(9/11 Terrorists' Attacks) の直後に，米国務省 (the Department of State) は米国市民にイスラエル・ウエストバンク・ガザへの旅行をとりやめるよう警告 (travel warning) を出しました。テロによる米市民の犠牲者を出さないための措置です。海外旅行の前に，目的地の危険度レベルをチェックしましょう。下に「旅行客のホテルへの苦情調査報告」が英文でのせてあります。（　　）内の正しい語を○で囲んでみて下さい。

　　　According (to /in / for) a survey of 1,000 travelers (by/ over / at) Westin Hotels & Resorts, low water pressure <33 percent> (stops /steps/ tops) the list of bathroom complaints. Also (disagree / disagreeable /disagreement) are a dirty tub <31 percent>, and a shower (carton/ curtain /certain) that sucks in and touches you <20 percent>.

【語句】a survey of ～「～を対象としたアンケート調査」, complaints「苦情」。Alsoで始まる1文は，倒置の用法で，「主語」はa dirty tub, and a shower ～で，「動詞」がareとなり，「補語」が（　　　）内の単語。文末の関係代名詞thatの先行詞はa shower ～。

For Your Information

　旅行関連 'Quiz' に答えてみよう。①米国内の旅行産業売上高の85％を占め，毎年5000万人以上の米市民が訪れる人気♯1のスポットは？（ギャンブル場：ビーチ：遊園地）②2000年度の米国内で，出張ビジネスマンが最も利用したホテルのレベルは？（1流ホテル：2流ホテル：モーテル）③オーストラリアで最も有名な観光スポット (most popular attraction) は，世界最大の1枚岩エアーズロック（Ayers Rock:アボリジニー名はUluru）だが，年間この場所を訪れる観光客数はどの位？（50万人以上：100万人以上：150万人以上）

Traveling

6. *Violence Gene*

暴力的遺伝子

PART 1 SCIENCE TOPICS

DRD4遺伝子（DRD4 gene）が新しいモノ好き（novelty-seeking）を決定する遺伝子である，というイスラエルのリチャード・P・エブスタイン博士チームの報告が出されたのが1996年のことです。この発見が，人の遺伝子と人の性格は脳内の特定の信号伝達システムにより関連していることを示唆（しさ）する，最初の手がかりになったのです。脳内細胞は，ドーパミン（dopamine）と呼ばれる化学伝達物質が，細胞間の伝令役をつとめます。ドーパミンは信号を送る細胞が出す化学物質で，信号を受けとる細胞表面にある受容体（receptor）にくっつき，メッセージを伝えます。研究の結果，特定の遺伝子が細胞に対し，1種類のドーパミン受容体を作る指示を出すことが判りました。また，DRD4特殊型遺伝子を持つ人は，持たない人に比べて，平均して10パーセント新しいモノ好きな傾向を示すことも判りました。

VOCABULARY

▶ **Choose the word that has the same meaning as the underlined one.**

1. Gaining 11 to 18 pounds doubles the <u>risk</u> of developing Type II diabetes.
   a. action   b. exposure to danger   c. something good

2. Your <u>career</u> sounds exciting.
   a. occupation   b. opportunity   c. organization

3. What does the <u>genome</u> mean to you?
   a. the complete set of genetic material
   b. the complete set of works
   c. the complete set of artistic material

LISTENING

▶ **Listen to the tape, and mark your answers.**

1. Mark your answer on your answer sheet.   Ⓐ Ⓑ Ⓒ

2. Mark your answer on your answer sheet.   Ⓐ Ⓑ Ⓒ

3. Mark your answer on your answer sheet.   Ⓐ Ⓑ Ⓒ

4. Mark your answer on your answer sheet.   Ⓐ Ⓑ Ⓒ

5. Mark your answer on your answer sheet.   Ⓐ Ⓑ Ⓒ

6. Mark your answer on your answer sheet.   Ⓐ Ⓑ Ⓒ

7. Mark your answer on your answer sheet.   Ⓐ Ⓑ Ⓒ

Check it out!

　リスニングのPart Ⅱ：「応答問題」は，くり返し言いますが，問題文・選択肢とも「すべて音声」のみで進行します。試験会場で配布されるテストブックのこのパートには，'Mark your answer on your answer sheet.' という短文以外に，目で確認しヒントとなる印刷文はありません。

　さらには，他のパート，つまり Part Ⅰ / Part Ⅲ / Part Ⅳ は，Ⓐ Ⓑ Ⓒ Ⓓ の中から正解を1つ塗りつぶす4択方式なのに対し，Part Ⅱだけは Ⓐ Ⓑ Ⓒ から正解を特定する3択方式だということ。パート別のテスト形式を，あらかじめ情報とし理解しておけば，精神的な負担を軽くし，これから迎える問題にうまく集中できるようになります。

Violence Gene

READING

▶ Read the following passage and answer the questions after it. Questions #1 and #2 test your comprehension. In Question #3, choose the answer that best completes the sentence. In Question #4, find the error in the sentence.

Recently, scientists have decoded the human genome. The genome is the DNA code for making a human being. The code is written in genes made of nucleotides. Now that we can read it, many researchers are looking for the causes of human behavior. We know that some kinds of behavior seem to be inherited. One study, in 1993, found a connection between aggressive behavior and genes. An abnormal gene on the X chromosome caused an imbalance of certain brain chemicals. Those with the gene were often more impulsive. They did things without thinking much about the consequences. Our genes don't control our lives completely, but they seem to push us towards making certain kinds of choices. Some people just like danger, so they are more likely to do risky things. In the end, life may be just like a card game. We can't control which cards we get, but how we play is up to us.

1. How did the abnormal gene found on the X chromosome affect behavior?
   (A) It caused people to be sad and depressed.
   (B) It was the cause of mountain climbing accidents.
   (C) It caused an increase in some types of risky behavior.
   (D) It resulted in an increase in cautious behavior and attitudes.
   　Ⓐ Ⓑ Ⓒ Ⓓ

2. What do scientists think determines our habits and behavior in life?
   (A) Genetics control everything about our behavior.
   (B) Our life experience is the only important factor.
   (C) Our personal attitudes are the result of luck and chance.
   (D) Our behavior is a combination of genetics and experience.
   　Ⓐ Ⓑ Ⓒ Ⓓ

3. Compulsive gamblers are more _____ in the risk than they are in the money.
   (A) excited (B) enjoying (C) interested (D) gambling
   　Ⓐ Ⓑ Ⓒ Ⓓ

4. It is almost <u>impossible</u> to <u>became</u> very successful <u>without</u> taking <u>a few</u> chances.
   　　　　　　　　(A)　　　　(B)　　　　　　　　　(C)　　　　(D)　　Ⓐ Ⓑ Ⓒ Ⓓ

PART 2 RELATED ARTICLE

リチャード・P・エブスタイン博士チームの発見した「新しいモノ好き遺伝子」の愛称は，'fad gene' といいます。それでは，この遺伝子にまつわる続編といえる記事をのせてみましょう。下線部の同意語，もしくは説明文を，ⓐ～ⓔの中から1つずつ捜し出してみて下さい。

In the process of discovering the dopamine receptor gene DRD4, researchers found it was
　　　　①　　　　　　　　　　　　　　　　　　　　②
associated with novelty-seeking type of personality. People scoring high in this
　③
trait are impulsive, fickle ,excitable, quick-tempered and extravagant. Those scoring
　④
low tend to be reflective , rigid, loyal , stoic, slow to anger and frugal.
　　　　　　　　　　　　　　　　　　　⑤

　ⓐ unit of heredity which is transferred from a parent to offspring.
　ⓑ connected.
　ⓒ a series of actions towards achieving a particular end.
　ⓓ enduring pain and hardship without complaining.
　ⓔ a distinguishing quality.

【語句】genes (which are) associated with ～ have also been found の1文では，「主語」が genes，「述部」が have also been found。People scoring high = People who score high「この遺伝子の特長を強く持つ人々」

For Your Information

　gene「遺伝子」とは，ギリシャ語の pan-「すべて」＋ genos「人類；子孫」という意味で，結局，遺伝の究極の単位，ということ。健康・栄養・アルコール・ニコチン・薬品など，ありとあらゆる医学情報を手に入れられるホームページに 'Go Ask Alice' がある。
http://www.goaskalice.columbia.edu/index.html

Violence Gene

7. Smart Buildings

ハイテクビル

PART 1 SCIENCE TOPICS

ある人が'smart'だといえば、「頭の切れる」という意味ですが、同じ'smart'を建物・兵器・機器に用いると「ハイテクの；高性能の」という意味になります。例えば、ディスプレー画面をみながら誘導する空対地ミサイルを「スマート爆弾」(smart bomb)といったり、メモリーチップを組み込んだカードを「スマートカード」(smart card)と呼びます。科学技術分野では、センサーや作動装置(actuator)を組み込み、高レベルの機能を達成するシステムを「スマート」ということに注意しましょう。

また、ハイテク素材(smart materials)は、橋・ダム・沖合い原油掘削やぐら(offshore oil-drilling tower)・電柱(utility pole)といった土木工学(civil engineering)にも活かされています。光ファイバー感知器(fiber-optic sensor)を必要箇所に埋めこみ、問題箇所を特定するなど、重要な役割をはたしています。

VOCABULARY

▶ Write the English words that correspond to following Japanese words.

1. ひずみ →s_____ 2. 損害を与える →d_____
3. 改築する →r_____ 4. ガレージ →g_____
5. 腐食（ふしょく）→c_____

LISTENING

▶ Listen to the tape, and mark your answers.

1. What does the man conclude about the cost of the strain sensors?

    (A) Building maintenance costs will increase.

    (B) They are worth the cost over the long-term.

    (C) They will not increase the cost of construction.

    (D) It is more important to save money on construction.

    Ⓐ Ⓑ Ⓒ Ⓓ

2. What does the woman decide is necessary?

    (A) A sensor review.

    (B) A weather forecast.

    (C) A damage assessment.

    (D) A new structural design.

    Ⓐ Ⓑ Ⓒ Ⓓ

3. Why did the woman think the building was younger than it really is?

   (A) It is built in a modern style.
   (B) It is in surprisingly good condition.
   (C) The guide told her it was not very cold.
   (D) It's really only a couple of years older than she thought.   Ⓐ Ⓑ Ⓒ Ⓓ

4. Which does the man think they should do?

   (A) Build a new office building.
   (B) Remodel the current building.
   (C) Save money by doing nothing.
   (D) Move the office to another building.   Ⓐ Ⓑ Ⓒ Ⓓ

5. What is the woman concerned about?

   (A) How much the bridge will cost.
   (B) Whether the public will like the bridge.
   (C) How long the bridge is expected to last.
   (D) Who will supervise operation of the bridge.   Ⓐ Ⓑ Ⓒ Ⓓ

― *Check it out !* ―

　Part Ⅲ「会話問題」を高速で処理し，スコアをあげるには，なんといってもテストブックに印刷されている質問文にあらかじめ目を通すことが重要です。特に <When /Where /What /Why /Who /How> という疑問詞を意識し，問題点をつかむことが大切です。そしてその後に音声で流される「2人の会話文」の内容を予測するようにしましょう。最初は難しいかもしれませんが，練習をくり返すことで，徐々に確実に手ごたえを感じられるようになってきます。すべては，一定量のトレーニングが出来を決めるといっても過言ではありません。

Smart Buildings 　33

READING

▶ Read the following passage and answer the questions after it. Questions #1 and #2 test your comprehension. In Question #3, choose the answer that best completes the sentence. In Question #4, find the error in the sentence.

High-Tech Structure

Buildings have always been designed to be strong, but not to be smart. They can't tell us when they have a problem. They can break suddenly. Buildings can fall down and bridges can collapse. There are many ways to check for trouble, but someone has to go and look for it. It's expensive and it takes a long time to check an entire structure. Some parts are very difficult to inspect. Recently, however, engineers are finding ways to put tiny sensors inside the materials they use to build. The high-tech polymers and crystals, fiber optic cables and other sensors constantly monitor the health of the structure. They can report any damage caused by age or corrosion. Finding problems early and fixing them before they get bigger can save a lot of money. It can also save lives. As the sensors become cheaper, many of the basic things we use in daily life will become smarter.

1. What do engineers usually do now to monitor buildings?
   (A) They don't monitor them at all.
   (B) They go to the site and check them.
   (C) They use sophisticated computer programs to watch them.
   (D) They analyze data from earthquakes to see if repairs are needed.

2. How are basic building materials changing?
   (A) They are becoming stronger.
   (B) They becoming much smaller and cheaper.
   (C) They are becoming more vulnerable to damage.
   (D) They are being designed to monitor themselves.

3. The freezing and thawing of winter weather _____ roads in northern climates.
   (A) damages   (B) repairing   (C) destroy   (D) cracking

4. Advanced <u>synthetic</u> materials will <u>allow</u> us <u>constructing</u> virtually <u>ageless</u> structures.
       (A)   (B)   (C)   (D)

PART 2 RELATED ARTICLE

ハイテク構造技術（smart structure technology）を応用した具体例をいくつがあげてみましょう。大手製薬会社 Pfizer ＜ファイザー＞では，イギリスのケント州に設立した新しい研究所で，温度・湿度・気圧を「光ファイバー技術」を使い制御してます。同様にカリフォルニア州のシリコン・バレーにあるサノゼ国際空港では，通信・コントロールシステムに光ファイバー技術を導入してます。また，米沿岸警備隊（U.S. Coast Guard）の砕氷船「ポーラースター号」（Polar Star）のスクリュー（propeller blade）には，54のファブリー・ペロー干渉計（Fabry-Perot interferometer）があり，これらに「光ファイバー技術」が使われています。

それでは，下の「検査指示票」（Inspection Order）の空所（1）～（5）に入るべき，適切な語句を下の ⓐ～ⓔ から1つずつ選び，埋めてみてください。

Inspection Order

(1) 02-3341　　　　　　　　　(4) Robert Simpkins
(2) 6/13/02　　　　　　　　　(5) 934-2938 ext.34

---

(3)　　Perform a visual and acoustic inspection of all supporting beams in the pedestrian walkway over Morrison Avenue. Photograph the current condition of the walkway surface for future assessment.

ⓐ Contact #　　ⓑ Authorized by　　ⓒ Work Order #
ⓓ Job Date　　ⓔ Job Description

【語句】Perform～「～を実施する」，acoustic「音波を使った」，a supporting beam「橋脚」，a pedestrian walkway「歩道橋」，over～「～にかかっている」，for future assessment「将来の査定目的用に」，#→「ナンバー」と読む

For Your Information

米 Citibank 銀行所有のニューヨークにある高層オフィスビル 'Citicorp Building' の屋上には，強風のショック・アブソーバー役をする400トンのコンクリート製厚板（slab）が置いてある。この「調節マスダンパー」（tuned mass damper: TMD）と呼ばれるシステムのおかげで，建物の横ゆれを最大40％も減らせる，というからモ・ノ・ス・ゴ・イ！

8. Asteroid Busting

小惑星爆発

PART 1 SCIENCE TOPICS

太陽のまわりを周回軌道をえがきながら彷徨（ほうこう）する小さな惑星，それが「小惑星」（minor planet）です。小惑星の大きさには，直径（diameter）が1000キロもあるセレス小惑星（Ceres）から，小さいものでは小石サイズのものまで様々あります。地球の軌道内に入り，土星へと周回する，直径240キロ以上ある小惑星は，現在のところ16観測されています。ただし，ほとんどの小惑星は火星と木星の軌道間内をグルグル回っています。また，小惑星の中には地球の大気圏に突入し，燃えつきた例も少なくありません。燃えつきずに残った小惑星で，最も保存状態のよいものの1つに，「バリンジャー隕石」（Barringer Meteor）があり，地表への衝突でできた「バリンジャー隕石クレーター」は，アリゾナ州のウィンズロー近くにあります。

VOCABULARY

▶ match the items in the two columns.

1. fiery   ・   ・ a. important
2. crash   ・   ・ b. relating to astronomy
3. astronomical ・   ・ c. colliding violently
4. major   ・   ・ d. consisting of fire
5. asteroid   ・   ・ e. a rocky body orbiting the sun

LISTENING

▶ Listen to the tape, and mark your answers.

Questions 1 and 2 refer to the following report.

1. How did the scientist know there had been an explosion?

   (A) He saw it.
   (B) He found clear evidence of it.
   (C) He was there when it happened.
   (D) He read the published news reports.

   Ⓐ Ⓑ Ⓒ Ⓓ

2. What did the pattern of the broken trees indicate?

   (A) That there was a large forest fire.
   (B) That something had hit the ground.
   (C) That an explosion had happened in the air.
   (D) That a huge crater had been made on the ground.

   Ⓐ Ⓑ Ⓒ Ⓓ

Question 3 and 4 refer to the following announcement.

3. What kind of information does this announcement present every month?

   (A) The Perseid metor showers.
   (B) The latest NASA Space Shuttle launch schedule.
   (C) The monthly nighttime weather and traffic forecast.
   (D) The most interesting astronomical sights for the month. Ⓐ Ⓑ Ⓒ Ⓓ

4. Why will August 11th probably be better for viewing the meteors than the 12th?

   (A) It will be cloudier on the 12th.
   (B) It will be easier to see them on the 11th.
   (C) There will be more of them on the 11th.
   (D) The showers will be in the Northern Hemisphere. Ⓐ Ⓑ Ⓒ Ⓓ

― *Check it out!* ―

　上にあげた「説明文問題」は、最初の例が107語構成で、平均的長さの問題、2つ目の例が81語構成で短めの問題です。最近の Part Ⅳ の問題は、音声を活字にすると、短いもので70語前後、長いもので120語前後です。そして、主流は、今、上でやっていただいた語い数幅におさまる問題で、しかも「関連問題2題型」とご理解下さい。まず、この100語前後の英文音声に抵抗がなくなるように「聴くことに慣れること」が大切です。そして、「ナニがどうなっているのか」をつかむことを最初の目標としましょう。すべては、練習と工夫、すべては志（こころざし）の高さにかかっていると言えます。

Asteroid Busting

READING

▶ Read the following passage and answer the questions after it. Questions #1 and #2 test your comprehension. In Question #3, choose the answer that best completes the sentence. In Question #4, find the error in the sentence.

Killer Asteroid

Every half a million years or so, an asteroid more than a kilometer across hits the Earth. One may have killed the dinosaurs. Even a smaller one could kill millions of people. Recently, the Near Earth Asteroid Tracking (NEAT) project is searching for large asteroids that cross the earth's path. They have found some that have passed quite close. Sometime in the future, they may find one coming straight at us. In Hollywood movies, astronauts are sent to destroy the asteroid with a nuclear bomb, but that may not be a good idea. It might just turn one big problem into hundreds of smaller problems. A better solution may be to deflect the asteroid while it is still far away. A slight change in either its speed or direction should be enough to make it miss the Earth. That makes projects like NEAT even more important. The sooner we detect an asteroid, the easier it will be to deflect it away from us.

1. What is the purpose of the NEAT project?
    (A) To blow up Hollywood studios.
    (B) To look for dangerous asteroids.
    (C) To deflect asteroids away from earth.
    (D) To cause the extinction of the dinosaurs.

2. Why isn't Hollywood's nuclear bomb plan a good solution?
    (A) It is too expensive.
    (B) It is impossible to send a bomb.
    (C) It might break the asteroid up into many pieces.
    (D) It would just make the asteroids come faster.

3. Stones found on top of glaciers often _____ to be fragments of meteorites.
    (A) time off   (B) turn out   (C) tone up   (D) tune in

4. With powerful new telescopes researchers can finally learn more for asteroids.
    (A)   (B)   (C) (D)

PART 2 RELATED ARTICLE

小惑星は，太陽系 (the solar system) が誕生し形成する時にとり残された物質で，惑星になりそこなった物質から出来ていると考えられています。地球に衝突する小惑星を「隕星体」(meteoroid) と呼び，地球圏内に突入し高速の大気摩擦により光を発しながら流れていくと「流星」(meteor) となり，燃えつきずに地上にたどりついたものを「隕石」(meteorite) と呼んでいます。これまで入手した隕石を分析した結果，構成物の92.8パーセントは珪酸塩 (silicate)，5.7パーセントは鉄とニッケルと判明しています。それではこれに関連した問題に取り組んでみましょう。(　　) 内の単語を適正な形に変え，文法的に整合性をもつようにしてみてください。

　　Because asteroids are made of material from the very early solar system, scientists are (interest) in their (compose). Spacecraft that have (fly) through the asteroid belt have (find) that the belt is really quite empty and that asteroids are (separate) by very large distances.

【語句】spacecraft「宇宙探査機」は複数名詞として扱う。そして同語で始まるこの１文は，「主語」がspacecraft,「動詞」がhave (find), 目的語に相当する名詞節はthat the belt is really quite emptyとand that asteroids are 〜 distancesの２つ。

For Your Information

　1990年までは，小惑星に関する情報収集は地球ベースに限られていたが，1991年10月，転機が訪れた。宇宙探査機「ガリレオ」が宇宙に乗り出し初めて小惑星「951ガスプラ」(951 Gaspra) に接近し，高解像度写真 (hi-resolution images) の撮影に成功した。ガリレオはまた，1993年８月に，２つ目の小惑星「243アイダ」(243 Ida) への接近にも成功している。1997年６月27日，宇宙探査機「ニア」(NEAR) は，小惑星「253マチルデ」(253 Mathilde) との高速接近に成功した。

9. Emerging Diseases

新種の病気

PART 1 SCIENCE TOPICS

代表的な新種の病気に，エボラ出血熱（Ebola fever）・ヒト免疫不全ウィルス（HIV）・C型肝炎(hepatitis C)・ハンタウィルス（hanta virus）・A型インフルエンザ（influenza A virus）などがあります。エボラ出血熱が最初に発生したのは1976年，その原因がウィルスと判明したのは翌1977年のことです。これまで，コートジボアール共和国・コンゴ共和国・ガボン共和国・スーダン共和国の4カ国で発症が確認されており，致死率が高いことで知られています。サルが感染源と考えられていますが，「アジア種エボラウィルス」（Asian-strain Ebola-Reston）に感染しているサルの場合は，今のところ，人にエボラ出血熱を発症させた報告例はありません。

エイズの原因となるＨＩＶウィルス（human immunodeficiency virus）が，最初に分離されたのが1983年。エイズが発生して以来，世界中の感染者は3060万人，エイズもしくはエイズ関連疾病（しっぺい）で亡くなった人は約1200万人と見積もられています。

VOCABULARY

▶ Choose the word that has the same meaning as the underlined one.

1. All the workers here are supposed to wear safety glasses.

    a. protective goggles   b. I.D. card   c. protective helmets

2. Do you know who invented the telescope?

    a. mirrors   b. optical instrument   c. image

3. West Nile virus was first confirmed to be in the United States in 1999.

    a. submicroscopic infective particle
    b. tropical disease
    c. subtropical diseases

LISTENING

▶ Listen to the tape, and mark your answers.

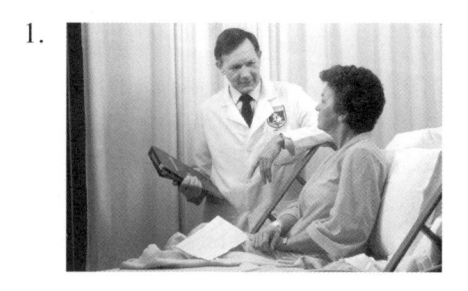

1.

Ⓐ Ⓑ Ⓒ Ⓓ

2.

Ⓐ Ⓑ Ⓒ Ⓓ

3.

Ⓐ Ⓑ Ⓒ Ⓓ

4.

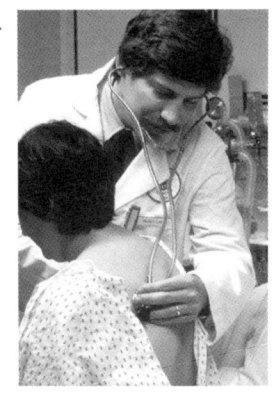

Ⓐ Ⓑ Ⓒ Ⓓ

5.

Ⓐ Ⓑ Ⓒ Ⓓ

6.

Ⓐ Ⓑ Ⓒ Ⓓ

Check it out !

　Part Ⅰ「写真描写問題」の解答時間は，1問につき「5秒」です。試験会場ではこの5秒を使って，アンサーシートの該当番号 Ⓐ–Ⓓ の中から，正解と思われる1つを黒く塗りつぶすことになります。このパートで確実にスコアをゲットするコツは，「事前に写真を見る→音声による Ⓐ–Ⓓ の短文が読まれる→終了とともに正解を塗りつぶす作業を2秒で完了→次問の写真をしっかり見る」という手順を完全に身につけることです。手順＝戦略，とお考え下さい。

Emerging Diseases

READING

▶ Look at the following data and answer the questions after it. Questions #1 and #2 test your comprehension. In Question #3, choose the answer that best completes the sentence. In Question #4, find the error in the sentence.

The History of Known Ebola Cases in Humans to 1996

Year	Ebola species	Country	No. of cases	Percentage of deaths
1976	Ebola-Zaire	Zaire	318	88%
1976	Ebola-Sudan	Sudan	284	53%
1976	Ebola-Sudan	England	1	0%
1979	Ebola-Sudan	Sudan	34	65%
1994	Ebola-Zaire	Gabon	44	63%
1994	Ebola-Ivory Coast	Ivory Coast	1	0%
1995	Ebola-Zaire	Zaire	315	81%
1996	Ebola-Zaire	Gabon	37	57%
1996	Ebola-Zaire	Gabon	60	75%
1996	Ebola-Zaire	South Africa	2	50%

1. Where did the first known case of Ebola occur?

    (A) South Africa
    (B) Gabon
    (C) Zaire
    (D) Ivory Coast   Ⓐ Ⓑ Ⓒ Ⓓ

2. When was the only known case of Ebola outside of Africa reported?

    (A) 1976
    (B) 1979
    (C) 1994
    (D) 1996   Ⓐ Ⓑ Ⓒ Ⓓ

3. Quarantine is the only effective way to stop _____ of some new viral diseases.

    (A) diseased
    (B) outbreaks
    (C) incidental
    (D) happening   Ⓐ Ⓑ Ⓒ Ⓓ

5. Viruses that mutate quickly can sometimes jump from one species to other.
             (A)   (B)   (C)   (D)

                                                                 Ⓐ Ⓑ Ⓒ Ⓓ

PART 2 RELATED ARTICLE

この課の冒頭で採り上げた，残り３つの病気について簡単に触れておきましょう。「Ｃ型肝炎」は1989年にウィルスが原因と特定され，ほとんどの場合，輸血 (post-transfusion) によるものです。日・米・欧の輸血肝炎の約９割はＣ型肝炎です。「ハンタウィルス」が米南部諸州で発生したのが1993年のことで，ウィルスによる致死率の高い呼吸器系感染症 (highly fatal respiratory disease) です。カナダ・南米でも症例が報告されています。「Ａ型インフルエンザ」のウィルスは，鳥によくみかける病原菌 (pathogen) で，人の身体からこのウィルスを初めて分離したのが1997年のこと。当初，大規模な流行病になるかと心配されましたが，予想外に感染力が弱く，1997年に鎮圧されました。それでは，ここで問題です。下にあげた５つの箇条書き英文を読み「ふさわしいタイトル」を@～@の中から，１つ選びましょう。

Your Chosen Title Here

- Use latex gloves when handling suspected biohazard material.
- Place the biohazard material inside an orange biohazard bag. Remove contaminated gloves and place in the bag.
- Tie the biohazard bag and place in a white biohazard transport container.
- Wash hands with the anti-microbial green soap found in the restrooms for at least 30 seconds, scrubbing thoroughly, and rinse well.
- Contact Environmental Health and Safety Services (846-2043) to schedule an appointment to have the biohazard material picked up for proper disposal.

ⓐ Disposal Procedures for Suspected Biohazard Material
ⓑ How To Use Latex Gloves
ⓒ Using White Biohazard Transport Containers
ⓓ Scheduling An Appointment Is A Must for Proper Disposal

For Your Information

バクテリア (bacteria) が原因の病気に，レジオネラ菌が引きおこす「在郷軍人病」(Legionnaires' disease) / 大腸菌 (E.coli) が引きおこす「Ｏ157」/ ボレリア菌が引きおこす「ライム病」(Lyme disease) / ビブリオ属コレラ菌が引きおこす「Ｏ139」などがある。

10. Atlantic Heat Conveyor Currents

大西洋暖流コンベヤー

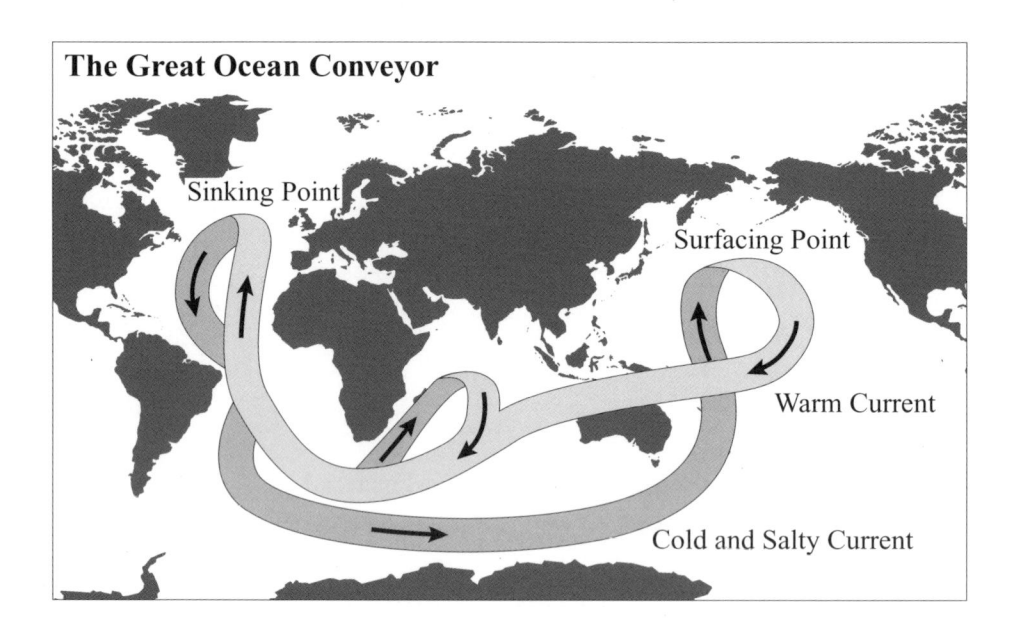

PART 1 SCIENCE TOPICS

コロンビア大学ラモント/ドハーティ地球観測所の地球環境科学科教授ワラス・S・ブロエッカーが，「大海洋コンベヤー理論」(the theory of the great ocean conveyor) を発表したのは1980年代後半のことでした。同理論とは，温室効果ガスの蓄積 (the buildup of greenhouse gases) は，太平洋・大西洋などの大海洋の潮流を急激に変化しうる，というものです。もし，そういう事態になれば，北大西洋地域の冬季の温度が，10年内に華氏で20度以上も下がると，ブロエッカー教授は予測しています。アイルランドの首都ダブリンの温度が，北極圏 (the Arctic Circle) の600マイル北にあるノルウェー領の島スピッツベルゲンと同じ寒さになることを意味します。なお，「コンベヤー」(the Conveyor) とは，地球規模で相互にリンクする深層海洋潮流のことで，地球上の熱や湿気を搬送することにより地球の気候を左右するのです。

VOCABULARY

▶ Write the English words that correspond to following Japanese words.

1. セーター →s＿＿＿＿＿＿＿＿
2. 衛　星 →s＿＿＿＿＿＿＿＿
3. 海　底 →ocean b＿＿＿＿＿
4. 表　面 →s＿＿＿＿＿＿＿＿
5. 彫　刻 →s＿＿＿＿＿＿＿＿

LISTENING

▶ Listen to the tape, and mark your answers.

1. Mark your answer on your answer sheet.　　　　　　Ⓐ Ⓑ Ⓒ

2. Mark your answer on your answer sheet.　　　　　　Ⓐ Ⓑ Ⓒ

3. Mark your answer on your answer sheet.　　　　　　Ⓐ Ⓑ Ⓒ

4. Mark your answer on your answer sheet.　　　　　　Ⓐ Ⓑ Ⓒ

5. Mark your answer on your answer sheet.　　　　　　Ⓐ Ⓑ Ⓒ

6. Mark your answer on your answer sheet.　　　　　　Ⓐ Ⓑ Ⓒ

7. Mark your answer on your answer sheet.　　　　　　Ⓐ Ⓑ Ⓒ

― *Check it out!* ―

　PartⅡの正解テクニックの1つは，疑問詞 <When「いつ」/ Where「どこで」/ What「何が」/ Why「なぜ」/ Who「だれが」/ Which「どっちが」/ How「どのように」> …でスタートする「疑問文」を正しく聴きとることです。例えば次のような文を見てみましょう。

- When will Ms. Thornton start her job?
- Where is the concert being held?
- What is your sales policy?
- Why is the print not so clear?
- Who is handling this job?
- Which do you like better, this red one or that blue one?
- How did you know I got a promotion?

重要なのは文の冒頭をよく聴きとることです。パート2の設問の「半分は疑問詞で始まる疑問文」ですから，意識的に練習し，慣れるようにしましょう。

Atlantic Heat Conveyor Currents

READING

▶ Read the following passage and answer the questions after it. Questions #1 and #2 test your comprehension. In Question #3, choose the answer that best completes the sentence. In Question #4, find the error in the sentence.

Britain is famous for gardens and golf, not for snow. Yet, Britain is as far north as Canada, Scandinavia and much of Russia. Though the climate is cool, it isn't as cold as those countries. That's because ocean currents keep it warm. Cold, salty water from the Arctic Sea is very heavy. It sinks deep to the ocean bottom and flows south. That pushes lighter, warmer water from the tropical seas north along the surface. This "heat conveyor" raises winter temperatures in Northern Europe five to ten degrees Celsius. It has made Europe more comfortable for humans, but it isn't very reliable. Scientists have found that the conveyor has stopped in the past. If global warming melts the ice caps, and lots of fresh water pours into the North Atlantic Ocean, the conveyor could again stop flowing. Warm water would no longer flow north, and Britain would probably become more famous for ice sculptures than for its flowers.

1. What do Britain, Canada, Scandinavia and Russia have in common?

    (A) They all have extremely cold winters.
    (B) All four are equally far north of the equator.
    (C) They are well known for their beautiful gardens.
    (D) They are all countries where English is the native language.

2. How does the heat conveyor affect the weather in Northern Europe?

    (A) It raises the temperature enough to make the winter warmer.
    (B) It causes the winter season to be longer, darker and much colder.
    (C) It increases the amount of snow and ice in countries near the equator.
    (D) It decreases the length of the summer season.

3. The earth's climate has often changed dramatically _____ its history.

    (A) once   (B) while   (C) about   (D) during

4. The repeated <u>advanced</u> and <u>retreat</u> of glaciers has <u>shaped</u> the land in <u>temperate</u> regions.
                   (A)   (B)   (C)   (D)

PART 2 RELATED ARTICLE

ブロエッカー教授説によると,「コンベヤー」のバランスは微妙で外部要因の影響を受けやすく, 地球が誕生以来, 何度も深層潮流がストップしたり, 方向転換したということです。そして, そのつど, 10年内に大規模な気温変化・風向変化・大気中のホコリ変化・氷河の前進/後退 (glacial advances or retreats) などの現象が, 地球上のいたるところでみられた, と主張しています。それではここで, 教授説の続きをのせてみますから, 日本語対応訳をヒントに, 空所の（ ）に1語を入れてみて下さい。例：(c   ) <寒い>→cold

　　　Today, the (d　　　) force <原動力> of the Conveyor is the cold, (s　　　) <塩分の濃い> water of the North Atlantic Ocean. Such water is (d　　　) <より密度が高い> than warm, fresh water and hence sinks to the ocean (b　　　) <海底>, pushing water through the world's oceans like a great plunger. The volume of this deep undersea (c　　　) <潮流> is 16 times greater than the (f　　　) <流れ> of all the world's rivers combined.

【語句】hence「その結果」, pushing = which (= such water) pushes
a great plunger「巨大な滝」, volume「水量」

─ *For Your Information* ─

　カナダの大西洋沖合いで, 塩分の濃い大量の水が大瀑布（だいばくふ）となり海底に沈み, ずっと南下し, 南米先端の沖合いから太平洋海底に抜け, さらに直進しアフリカ南端沖合いに達し, ここで, 南極を回遊する海底潮流と合体する。そこで海底潮流「コンベヤー」は, 海氷水で造られた冷たい塩分濃度の高い潮流でエネルギーを充電し, 北極をめざし北へ進路をとる。また, 南極回遊潮流は徐々にあたためられ, 太平洋・インド洋の表面へと浮かんでいく。北極をめざし北上した深層海流は北極から北米先端沖合いを通り, なんと1000年という長い歳月をかけて, 再びスタート地点のカナダ沖の大瀑布へ戻り深層回遊の旅を終える。休む間もなく潮流は, 新たな回遊の旅につくことになる。

11. Unexceptional Beauty

絶世の美人

PART 1 SCIENCE TOPICS

世界の歴代の美女といえば、クレオパトラ・楊貴妃（ようきひ）・小野小町（おののこまち）ということになっています。人は進化の過程を通し、「顔と肉体」が最も健康な繁殖 (most suitably fit for healthy reproduction) の適性基準で、これをベースに異性を「最も美しい」と脳が判断するように仕組まれているようです。「ルックスがいいこと」(good looks) は、健康であまり病気にならない代名詞と考えられていました。心理学者のディビッド・バスは、異文化研究 (cross-cultural study) を行い、魅力的で健康的なルックスを最重視する文化圏では、寄生虫性の病気 (parasitic diseases) が多い、と興味ある報告をしています。実は、同じような現象が、多くの色あざやかな鳴鳥（めいちょう：songbird）にもみかけられます。鳥類学者 (ornithologists) は、色あざやかさは「健康」のシンボルで、同時に最も寄生虫の多い種 (species) でもあると指摘しています。

VOCABULARY

Match the items in the two columns.

1. amazing ・　　　　・ a. surprising
2. unique ・　　　　・ b. change from one image to another
3. head ・　　　　・ c. act as the boss of
4. fair ・　　　　・ d. unlike anything else
5. morph ・　　　　・ e. treating people equally

LISTENING

▶ Listen to the tape, and mark your answers.

1. What did the woman think of Bob's eyes?

    (A) She thought his eyes were really brown.
    (B) She thought his eyes were naturally blue.
    (C) She thought he would look better with glasses.
    (D) She thought he was clever to wear contact lenses.   Ⓐ Ⓑ Ⓒ Ⓓ

2. Where did this conversation probably take place?

    (A) At a theater.
    (B) In an office.
    (C) At a restaurant.
    (D) In a supermarket.   Ⓐ Ⓑ Ⓒ Ⓓ

3. What advice does the man give to the woman?

   (A) He doesn't share his opinion with her.
   (B) He tells her not to change her nose at all.
   (C) He says she should have an operation on her nose.
   (D) He says she would look better with a different nose.　　Ⓐ Ⓑ Ⓒ Ⓓ

4. Why does the woman think of the man's appearance?

   (A) She thinks he looks fine.
   (B) She's not sure if his clothes are appropriate.
   (C) She wishes he were not dressed so conservatively.
   (D) She wonders if he needs more color in his wardrobe.　　Ⓐ Ⓑ Ⓒ Ⓓ

5. What are they discussing?

   (A) Their dissatisfaction with their jobs.
   (B) The qualifications of their new boss.
   (C) Their chances of promotion to the top job.
   (D) The candidates for the department head's job.　　Ⓐ Ⓑ Ⓒ Ⓓ

Check it out !

　Part Ⅲ「会話問題」の正答率を上げるには，音声を聴いて的確な状況判断するのはもちろん，同じ位重要なのが「手順」です。各問につき解答時間は8秒ありますから，「5秒」は解答に，残り「3秒」は次の設問スキャンに割りふる戦略が大切です。設問の事前読みが重要なのは，正解を絞り込むポイントを意識して重点的に聴くスタンスを確立できる点にあります。つまり，テストブックに 'When is this event taking place?' とあれば，When と event を意識し，音声放送 'X→Y→X' を待てばよいことになります。

Unexceptional Beauty

READING

▶ Read the following passage and answer the questions after it. Questions #1 and #2 test your comprehension. In Question #3, choose the answer that best completes the sentence. In Question #4, find the error in the sentence.

Beauty may be only skin deep, but it is still important. It's not fair, but attractive people have many advantages in life. Others often think they are smarter, more sociable and better at their jobs. Standards of beauty are different in different cultures, but they have some things in common. Beautiful people are those who look young and healthy, with no signs of disease or parasites. We often assume that the most attractive people, like supermodels and actors, are somehow special. They seem different than the rest of us, but they aren't. When photos of several average faces are morphed together with computer software, the result is usually considered more beautiful than any of the original photos. It is the average of a race or culture that is considered most attractive, not the exceptional. Beauty, it turns out, is generally just a collection of very ordinary parts.

1. How are attractive people treated by society in general?
   (A) They are treated the same as anyone else.
   (B) They are treated more harshly than average people.
   (C) They are not treated as well as unusual people are.
   (D) They are usually treated better than less attractive people.

2. Why are actors and models considered so attractive?
   (A) They have very ordinary faces.
   (B) They have strikingly unusual faces.
   (C) Their photos are in magazines often.
   (D) They look different than beautiful people.

3. Older workers often have _____ finding new jobs after they have been laid off.
   (A) hard (B) been (C) trouble (D) difficult

4. Songbirds use <u>brightly</u> colored feathers <u>to show</u> potential mates <u>then</u> they are <u>healthy</u>.
            (A)   (B)   (C)   (D)

PART 2 RELATED ARTICLE

専門家の調査研究で，３ヶ月の赤ちゃんでも，ルックスのよい人と悪い人の写真を並べておくと，ルックスのよい人の写真をジーッとながめている時間が長いことがわかっています。また，どの文化圏でも好まれる女性の美顔の特徴は，「小顔でアゴが小さめで，ほお骨 (cheekbones) が高く，唇がプクッとしていて (full lips)，笑顔が大きく，目が大きい」こと。

これに対し男性は，「たくましいアゴと力強いまゆを持ちながらも，女性的ともいえるソフトな顔立ち」とのこと。それではここで，下にあげるファッション・モデルの記事中の英文を参考に，下の日本語の文章を英訳してみて下さい。

High Fashion Modeling

Fashion models are hired through agencies, and the pay rate is the highest among all modeling jobs. Advertisers expect only top models for this type of work. Agencies typically choose only models with certain physical characteristics.

Age: Under 26 preferred.

Height: 5' 7" to 6' 0"

Weight: Proportional to height.

Other Characteristics: Long legs, especially from the floor to the knee. Women with good complexions and long necks are preferred.

① 理系の学部生は，就職説明会やインターネットを通して主に採用が決まる。

② すべてのコンピュータ関連職の中でも，暗号技術をもつ専門職の給与が一番高い。

③ 給与体系は仕事の中身と経験に応じて決定される。

For Your Information

「最も美しい顔立ち」とは，特定の文化・民族で「最大公約数的な顔の特徴」をそなえた顔，という専門家の報告があるのは興味深い。その理由は，環境への適応能力の高さ・健康の証明とみなされることによる。

12. Flight Simulators

模擬飛行訓練装置

PART 1 SCIENCE TOPICS

日常の銀行業務・一定期間の株式資産運用 (stock portfolio)・組み立てライン操業 (running of an assembly line)・病院/警備会社のスタッフ配置 (staff assignment)・模擬飛行訓練といった実際のシステムを，コンピュータを使い模擬演習することを「システムシュミレーション」(system simulation) といいます。学習・訓練・スキルアップ・調査などの目的で，コンピュータ・プログラム化した実際のシステムをモデル化したソフトを使い，素人（しろうと）や訓練生が天候・環境に左右されずに学習できるメリットは大きいと言えるでしょう。なお，合衆国では，子供に金銭感覚を小さい時から身につけさせるのが盛んで，インターネットを使って株式・債権 (stocks and bonds) の資産運用訓練を，ゲーム感覚で学習できます。そんなサイトの代表的なものの一つに，'The Young Investor' <http://www.younginvestor.com/> があります。ためしに，一度，アクセスしてみたらいかが？。

VOCABULARY

▶ Choose the word that has the same meaning as the underlined one.

1. The hurricane has sustained winds of 100 miles an hour.

    a. bearing   b. continuous   c. noting

2. Could you tell us how effectively you run your café?

    a. move   b. cause   c. manage

3. How well can you perform in virtual simulators?

    a. physically existing by software   b. physically impossible   c. mentally possible

LISTENING

▶ Listen to the tape, and mark your answers.

Questions 1 and 2 refer to the following report.

1. What kind of simulation is the man talking about?

    (A) A flight simulation.

    (B) A financial simulation.

    (C) A crash test simulation.

    (D) An architectural simulation.

2. What did the test find?

   (A) It didn't find any significant problems.

   (B) A small problem was found that is easily fixed.

   (C) It found a major problem that has to be fixed.

   (D) The full event simulation hasn't been completed yet.

Questions 3 and 4 refer to the following advertisement.

3. Who would be most likely to use this software?

   (A) A powerful CEO.

   (B) A restaurant owner.

   (C) A basketball coach.

   (D) A Fortune 500 company.

4. How would a business benefit by using this software?

   (A) They would be able to raise all their prices.

   (B) They could more effectively restructure their staff.

   (C) They could predict how changes will affect their business.

   (D) They would know how much profit they will make in the future.

Check it out !

　Part Ⅳ「説明文問題」は，リスニングのすべてのパートの中で「最もタフ」です。でも，200語/分の速い音声スピードに慣れ，ビジネス常識を新聞・雑誌・ＴＶで豊かにすることで，出題例が身近なものに感じられるようになります。この作業を毎日，10分でもいいので根気よく継続し，同時に，「戦略」も身につけましょう。Part Ⅳの音声による問題指示が流れる「40秒」を使い，テストブックに印刷されている関連問題をすばやくスキャンする→設問から音声放送の内容を予測する→設問の答えのヒントとなるキーワードを意識して聴く。この手順を，頭の中で納得するまでシュミレーションしてみて下さい。音声放送の単語・イディオム・内容を言い換えてあるテストブックの選択肢は，常に正解になりますので注意して聴きましょう。<例> 音声：manufacture the parts→テストブック選択肢：produce them ...が正解です。

Flight Simulators

READING

▶ Read the following passage and answer the questions after it. Questions #1 and #2 test your comprehension. In Question #3, choose the answer that best completes the sentence. In Question #4, find the error in the sentence.

A Simulator Can Be A Solution

Everyone makes mistakes when they are learning. It's part of the process. For students in school that's OK, but for pilots it's not. Their first mistake could easily be their last. So how do we let people learn from their mistakes, without killing themselves? One solution is the simulator. The first flight simulators were just airplanes attached to a flexible joint. When the wind blew across the wings the plane reacted as if it was flying. Of course, it only worked on very windy days. Now, computer simulators are so powerful that they are able to accurately recreate almost any flight situation. New pilots can learn the fundamentals of how to control an airplane. Experienced ones can practice dealing with bad weather or unexpected problems. Simulators are useful in many other fields, too. Surgeons can perform virtual operations, engineers can crash test car designs and architects can put their buildings through earthquakes and hurricanes. After all, practice makes perfect.

1. Why are simulators better than actual airplanes for flight training?

    (A) They can more accurately simulate training conditions.
    (B) It is safer to learn in a simulator than in an airplane up in the sky.
    (C) It is cheaper to train in a simulator because it doesn't need gasoline.
    (D) Learning on a computer is less realistic than it was in the past.

2. How do architects use simulators in the design of new buildings?

    (A) They test various painting methods to see how long they will take.
    (B) The use the simulator to order coffee while working on the design.
    (C) During earthquakes, the simulator can protect them from falling debris.
    (D) Simulators show them how their designs will do under extreme conditions.

3. Crash simulators have to accurately _____ the results of real accidents.

    (A) prepare   (B) predict   (C) unless   (D) without

4. The <u>first</u> computer crash test simulators <u>were</u> crude, <u>slow</u> and difficult <u>for</u> use.
      (A)   (B)   (C)   (D)

PART 2 RELATED ARTICLE

1979年，イリノイ大学電気工学科の院生ブルース・アートウィックが，初めて「模擬飛行訓練シュミレーター」を開発しました。彼の開発したプログラムを買い取り，1982年11月に商品化し販売したのがマイクロソフト社で，商品名は，'Microsoft Flight Simulator 1.01' です。同商品の最新バージョンが 'Microsoft Flight Simulator 2002' で，精度とリアリティをさらに更新したものになっています。また，5大会計事務所の，プライスウォーターハウス・クーパーズでは，社内の緊急問題解決班（Emergent Solutions Group）が，監理職用の「想定問題」(what-if scenarios) ソフトを開発し，様々な会計難問が演習できるシステムを立ち上げています。それではここで，「民間機訓練プログラム説明」の一部を採りあげてみます。（　）内の正解と思われる語を１つ，○で囲んでみて下さい。

　　Students (enrolled : enroll to) in the Airline Training Program will (get : make) the training that most employers require (for : at) commercial pilot certification. (Training : Train) includes both simulated (or : and) actual flight environments.

For Your Information

　　1983年以来，車の衝撃耐久度 (crashworthiness) の業務用シュミレーション・ソフトとして，世界で最も有名なのが ESI グループ社の販売する 'PAM-CRASH'。外科手術のバーチャル・ソフトとして知られるのが 'Boston Dynamics' Surgical Simulators'，都市開発・歴史上の古戦場シュミレーション・ソフトで No.1 の評価をえているのが，スィド・メイヤーの開発した 'Sim City' だ。

13. Return of the Mammoth

マンモスの再現

PART 1 SCIENCE TOPICS

氷河期（the Ice Age）の最も有名な哺乳動物（mammal）といえば何を思いうかべますか？マンモスですよね。これまで発掘された最古のマンモスといわれるのは，15万年前に，ユーラシア大陸のステップ地帯（the Steppes）に生息していた，第2氷河期後半（the second to the last glaciation）のトロゴンテリィ・マンモス（Mammuthus trogontherii）です。マンモスの姿形の大部分が判っている背景には，死体（carcasses）がシベリアの凍土（frozen ground）に保存された状態で数多く発見されたことや，欧州の古代洞窟壁画に描かれていたことがあげられます。もっとも保存のよい状態で発掘されたサンプルの一つに，カナダのユーコン準州にある，ホワイトストーン川で見つかったほぼマンモス一体分の骨があります。この骨は，放射性炭素年代測定（radiocarbon dating）で，3万年前のものと判っています。また，シベリアで1990年に発見された完全な氷づけのマンモスの死体は，サンクトペテルブルグ博物館に保存されています。

VOCABULARY

▶ Write the English words that correspond to following Japanese words.

1. スチーム → s _____
2. コンテナ → c _____
3. ラボ → l _____
4. フラスコ → f _____
5. チューブ → t _____

LISTENING

▶ Listen to the tape, and mark your answers.

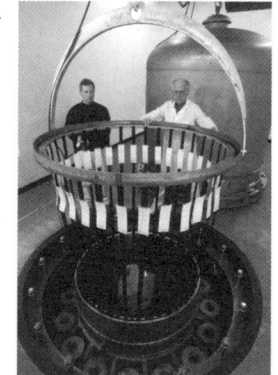

1. Ⓐ Ⓑ Ⓒ Ⓓ

2. Ⓐ Ⓑ Ⓒ Ⓓ

3.

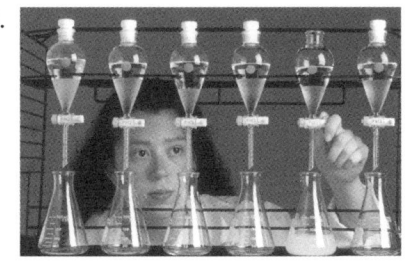

Ⓐ Ⓑ Ⓒ Ⓓ

4.

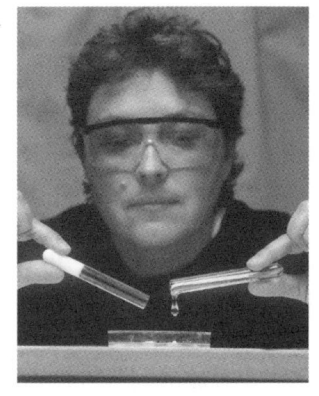

Ⓐ Ⓑ Ⓒ Ⓓ

5.

Ⓐ Ⓑ Ⓒ Ⓓ

6.

Ⓐ Ⓑ Ⓒ Ⓓ

Check it out!

　PartⅠの音声放送選択肢で正解になるのは,「人物／物」を描写する際に使われる「現在進行形」です。つまり,'be動詞＋ing'の形をとる現在進行形で,正解の「8割」がこの形です。具体的には,The airplane is going to take off.「飛行機はいま離陸しようとしているところです」 The woman is carrying heavy luggage.「女性は重いスーツケースを運んでいるところです」といった現在進行形が「正解の主役」だということを,十分ご理解下さい。

READING

▶ Read the following passage and answer the questions after it. Questions #1 and #2 test your comprehension. In Question #3, choose the answer that best completes the sentence. In Question #4, find the error in the sentence.

Cloning the Mammoth

Thousands of years ago, the mammoth walked the earth. It looked like a modern elephant, but it had long woolly hair. We occasionally find their bodies, frozen in glaciers or mud. Dinosaur fossils are made of stone. The original bones and flesh are long gone. But the frozen mammoths are preserved like a steak in a freezer. They still have DNA. With modern cloning technology, some scientists think we will be able recover DNA and bring the mammoth back to life. There are many problems with the idea. It is hard to find mammoth bodies that have stayed completely frozen for thousands of years. Usually, the DNA is badly damaged. Even with perfect DNA samples, cloning is difficult and often fails, but scientists are optimistic. If they succeed, the woolly mammoth may once again walk the earth.

1. Why can't dinosaurs be cloned from fossils?

    (A) Because fossils have no DNA to clone.
    (B) Because the DNA is too badly damaged.
    (C) Because they are too dangerous to bring back.
    (D) Because they have no closely related modern relatives.

2. How do scientists think they can clone mammoths?

    (A) By using fossils of ancient elephants.
    (B) They plan to clone DNA from preserved dinosaurs.
    (C) By recovering DNA from frozen mammoth bodies.
    (D) They think they can use frozen beef steak as a DNA source.

3. The _____ of the animal species in history have gone extinct.

    (A) most (B) many (C) much (D) majority

4. Cloning animals <u>have</u> not <u>been</u> as easy as many people <u>thought</u> it <u>would</u>.
                      (A)   (B)   (C)   (D)

PART 2 RELATED ARTICLE

「マンモス」は，急激な環境の変化に対処できなくなったのとあいまって，最後の氷河期の終わりにかけて，人間による捕獲（human predation）が盛んになると，どんどん個体数を減らしていきました。そして，約1万1000年前に，ほとんどのマンモスは絶滅したと考えられていました。ところが，1993年，驚くべき報告がありました。シベリア北東部沖にある島「ヴランゲリ島」で見つかった小型マンモス（dwarf woolly mammoths）を，放射性炭素測定したところ，今から7000年〜3700年前に生存していたことが判明したのです。なんと，古代エジプトの第3王朝（BC2500年）のピラミッドが設営された時代，イギリス南部で巨大な環状列石ストーンヘンジ（Stonehenge）が構築されたBC2500年〜2000年と同じ時期に，小型マンモスは北極海にある島でゆうゆう闊歩（かっぽ）していたとは！ ロマンあふれる話ですね。

ここで問題です。下にあげる説明文を読み，「ふさわしいタイトル」をⓐ〜ⓓの中から，1つ選んでみて下さい。

Your Chosen Title Here

Build a Skeleton: One way to teach basic structural anatomy to students is to put a skeleton back together.

Buy a whole chicken or turkey from a local butcher. Cook it normally and eat it. Then boil the bones in water and a small amount of ammonia. After several hours, the bones should be completely stripped of flesh. Dry them completely.

Depending on the age of the students, they can put the skeleton back together in a standing position with glue and wires or lay it out flat on a dark surface.

ⓐ Building A Mammoth Skelton
ⓑ Teaching Basic Human Anatomy To Students
ⓒ Cooking A Whole Chicken or Turkey
ⓓ Recommended Science Classroom Activities

For Your Information

mammothの発音は「ママス」で，語源はタタール語の mamma「地面」で，マンモスは地面に穴を掘って住むと考えられていたことによるらしい。

14. Echelon

エシュロン

PART 1 SCIENCE TOPICS

「エシュロン」とは，合衆国・英国・カナダ・オーストラリア・ニュージーランドの5カ国が共同運用する通信傍受システムのことです。世界中の一般通話・ファックス・eメールを日常的に傍受し，分析しているといわれています。当初は，ソ連を含む旧東側の情報を収集するのが目的でしたが，冷戦が終わった今日では，米英企業のビジネス活動の後方支援の手段に使われているといわれています。「いわれている」とは，共同運営している各国の国家安全保障局（National Security Agency）が，エシュロンの存在を公的に認めていないからです。でも，エシュロンにかつて勤務していたオーストラリア人が匿名でインタビューに応えたり，ドイツ・フランスなどの大手企業がどうみてもエシュロンによる諜報活動によるとしか思えないビジネス上の実害を何件か訴えていることから，実在しスパイ活動をしていることは事実のようです。

VOCABULARY

▶ Match the items in the two columns.

1. hacker   · · a. impossible to explain
2. properly   · · b. correctly
3. fire   · · c. dismiss from a job
4. mysterious   · · d. computer network intruder
5. intercept   · · e. obstruct

LISTENING

▶ **Listen to the tape, and mark your answers.**

1. Mark your answer on your answer sheet.　　　　　　　　Ⓐ Ⓑ Ⓒ

2. Mark your answer on your answer sheet.　　　　　　　　Ⓐ Ⓑ Ⓒ

3. Mark your answer on your answer sheet.　　　　　　　　Ⓐ Ⓑ Ⓒ

4. Mark your answer on your answer sheet.　　　　　　　　Ⓐ Ⓑ Ⓒ

5. Mark your answer on your answer sheet.　　　　　　　　Ⓐ Ⓑ Ⓒ

6. Mark your answer on your answer sheet.　　　　　　　　Ⓐ Ⓑ Ⓒ

7. Mark your answer on your answer sheet.　　　　　　　　Ⓐ Ⓑ Ⓒ

Check it out !

　Part Ⅱの質問の25％を占めるのが，'Is it ...? / Are you ...? / Did you ...? / Can they ...? / Has she ...?' などで始まる疑問文です。これを受ける「正解の応答文」は，Yes /Noで始まらない　ケースが，TOEIC®テストでは，標準形と理解しておいてください。'Yes / No' で始まり，正解となるケースでは，必ず次に「具体的な理由・根拠」が追加される場合に限られます。以下の具体例をご覧下さい。

① Q: Did you work overtime yesterday, Jill?
　正解の選択肢：I had to because the deadline is due this afternoon.「残業せざるをえなかったのよ。締め切りが今日の午後なものですから」

② Q: Are you busy now?
　正解の選択肢：No, what's on your mind?「いいえ，でも私に何か用ですか？」
　…いかがですか？最初はしっくりこないでしょうが，TOEIC方式の実践対話に慣れるようにがんばりましょう。

READING

▶ Read the following passage and answer the questions after it. Questions #1 and #2 test your comprehension. In Question #3, choose the answer that best completes the sentence. In Question #4, find the error in the sentence.

The U.S. National Security Agency (NSA) is the largest intelligence agency in the world. Many people are worried about a mysterious NSA project called "Echelon". Several countries are cooperating with them on it. It seems to be an effort to scan email, telephone, Internet and fax messages all over the world. The NSA has large stations in Europe, North America and Australia to intercept electronic signals. Huge computer systems are said to be filtering the world's signals looking for key words, phrases or names. NSA agents can then check the messages or calls for useful information. Some say Echelon is intercepting more than three billion messages a day and monitoring 90% of the Internet traffic. And that worries many people.

1. What is the NSA?
   (A) A secret government political party.
   (B) A multinational computer corporation.
   (C) A government intelligence organization.
   (D) A little known computer software virus.

2. How does Echelon work?
   (A) It destroys computer hard drives all over the world.
   (B) It searches through electronic communication signals.
   (C) It eliminates telephone calls, fax messages and private emails.
   (D) It prevents the transmission of Internet traffic between countries.

3. Communicating electronically is not always more _____ than by other ways.
   (A) safety
   (B) secure
   (C) safely
   (D) security

4. Email has become the preferred method for keeping on touch with clients.
                        (D)   (B)   (C)   (D)

PART 2 RELATED ARTICLE

エシュロン対策には，「ＰＧＰ暗号システム」(Pretty Good Privacy)が有効です。インターネットを使った，ｅメール・ファイルの送受信の機密保持のための標準化プログラムがＰＧＰです。このシステムは，1997年から2002年にかけて，「コンピュータ・プロの社会的使命」（ＣＰＳＲ）という研究委員会の特別委員長をつとめたフィル・ズィマーマンが考え出したものです。彼の考案した「公開鍵暗号方式」(public key cryptography system) のおかげで，面識のない相手に，暗号化したメッセージを送信し，またメッセージが本物であることを保障するでデジタル署名 (digital signature) をつけることが可能になったのです。それでは，問題です。下にあげた４つの短文は，「ＰＧＰ暗号ソフトのダウンロードの手順」を記したものですが，正しい手順にならべ換えてみて下さい。

ⓐ Click on the first download link under PGP Freeware v6.5.8 (Windows 95/98/NT/2000). You want to save this file to disk, so make sure this option is selected in the File Download dialog box, then click on O.K.

ⓑ Using your Internet browser, go to the download site at the Massachussetts Institute of Technology (MIT) : Distribution Center for PGP (Pretty Good Privacy) or go to the download center at PGP International and select the correct version of your Windows OS (98, 2000, ME, NT, etc.)

ⓒ Scroll down the page and click on the PGP Freeware Version 6.5.8.

ⓓ Be sure to select a location on your hard drive where later you'll be able to easily find the zip file of the PGP software, then click on the Save button.

(　　) → (　　) → (　　) → (　　)

For Your Information

　初期の暗号化は，暗号化法を秘密にしておく (security through obscurity) だけのものだったが，ＰＧＰは天文学的数字の中から１と０の組み合わせで構成される。数字の組み合わせが無限で複雑なことから「高性能コンピュータを駆使した解読作業」(brute force work) でも，解読する (decrypt ; read) のはほとんど不可能といわれる。1997年，３月20日，米国家安全保障局長代理のウィリアム・クロウウェル氏は次のような声明文を出した。「世界中のパソコンを動員したとしても，ＰＧＰ暗号化メッセージをたった１つ解読するのに，平均して，宇宙の年齢の1200万倍の時間がかかるだろう。」

15. Spider Ranching

クモの牧場化

PART 1 SCIENCE TOPICS

クモの糸(spider silk)は，同じ重さなら，鋼鉄よりも強い，といったら驚かれるかもしれません。クモの糸を鉛筆の太さに束ね大きなネットを作れば，飛行中のボーイング747機を受け止める程の強度があります。クモの糸の51％以上は，「フィブロイン」(fibroin)と呼ばれる繊維状の硬蛋白質（polymerized protein）で出来ています。クモは少なくても７つの目的別腺（glands）を持ち，作る糸の用途に応じて，異なる腺から排出される液を組み合わせ，糸のでき上がるスピードを調節し，量を決めていきます。また，円形網を張るクモ（orb-web spiders）にとって，糸のリサイクルは重要で，この種のクモはいとも簡単に再利用作業をやってのけます。悪天候や飛行中の獲物に，糸は簡単にこわされ，糸の粘着度（adhesiveness）も１〜２日でなくなります。でも，くもは古い糸を食べ，すぐに新しい糸に張りかえます。糸の切断・消化は，物理的には切断せずに，特殊な酵素（enzymes）を含む消化液で行い，クモはこの消化液を糸の繊維をくっつける時にも用いるのです。

VOCABULARY

▶ Choose the word that has the same meaning as the underlined one.

1. How did you think of a get-rich-quick scheme?
    a. fixing the date   b. decision-making   c. making quick money

2. What department are you with?
    a. dealing   b. division   c. district

3. It is the ranch owner who is demanding substantive change.
    a. dressing   b. large farm   c. large animal

LISTENING

▶ Listen to the tape, and mark your answers.

1. What are they discussing?

    (A) Job responsibilities.
    (B) Research techniques.
    (C) Industrial problems.
    (D) Musical instruments.

    Ⓐ Ⓑ Ⓒ Ⓓ

2. Why does the woman think the cables will be strong enough?

   (A) They are made from the most highly rated steel.
   (B) They're never been used under such a strain.
   (C) They are manufactured with specially designed alloys.
   (D) They are designed to support twice as much weight as required.　Ⓐ Ⓑ Ⓒ Ⓓ

3. How does the man expect the new golf club to improve his game?

   (A) It should improve his putting accuracy.
   (B) He hopes to correct his slicing problem.
   (C) He expects to be able to keep the ball on the fairway.
   (D) He will probably be able to hit the ball farther.　Ⓐ Ⓑ Ⓒ Ⓓ

4. How does the man plan to get rich?

   (A) By becoming a fishing guide.
   (B) By selling worms to fishermen.
   (C) By growing crops in Nebraska.
   (D) By inventing an earthmoving business.　Ⓐ Ⓑ Ⓒ Ⓓ

5. What does the man think of spiders?

   (A) He likes them.
   (B) He is terrified of them.
   (C) He thinks they are very useful.
   (D) He doesn't know about the spider.　Ⓐ Ⓑ Ⓒ Ⓓ

Check it out !

　PartⅢ：「会話問題」の正答率を上げるには，「手順」が大切なことを11課でふれました。今回はテストブックに印刷されている「設問文の疑問詞」の「どこに集中して」音声を聴けばよいか記してみましょう。
▷Where ＜X→Y→Xの対話から，「場所」を絞る。一番簡単な出題例が多いが，まれに「場所の変更」を連絡するタイプのちょっとひねったケースもある＞　▷When ＜曜日・時間・月・年度に注意を払い「いつ」かを特定する。時には，対話中の月が8月で，2ヶ月後にイベントがある→Q：イベントはいつ？式の，ちょっとした算数を求める出題例もある＞　▷Why ＜主として，X→Y→X の発言のうち，最後の X の発言が「理由」の具体的ヒントになる出題例が多い＞ … Who / How は次回19課にゆずることにしましょう。

Spider Ranching

READING

▶ Read the following passage and answer the questions after it. Questions #1 and #2 test your comprehension. In Question #3, choose the answer that best completes the sentence. In Question #4, find the error in the sentence.

Have you ever tried to milk a spider? It's not easy. That's the problem scientists have when they try to use spider silk. The silk is one of nature's most amazing materials. It is thin, light and flexible, but extremely strong. Scientists can imagine many engineering uses for the silk, but a spider makes only a small amount. It is hard to get enough silk. Spiders make several different kinds of silk. The strongest kind is called dragline silk. It is made from two simple amino acids, but they combine in a complex way. Now, the U.S. Army and a Canadian biotechnology firm have a way to use gene-splicing technology to get spider silk from goats. They put spider's genes into the goat's DNA. The goats make spider silk in their milk. It still isn't as strong as natural spider silk, but the scientists expect it to get better as they learn more. And it is certainly easier than trying to manage a spider ranch.

1. Why is spider silk useful?
   (A) It is very sticky.
   (B) It is naturally white.
   (C) It is light and strong.
   (D) It is cheap and easy to produce.

2. How do the goats make spider silk?
   (A) They are crossbred with spiders.
   (B) Their DNA has spider's genes in it.
   (C) Their hair is very similar to spider silk.
   (D) They are very closely related to spiders.

3. Many advanced engineering techniques can also be _____ in nature.
   (A) found
   (B) shown
   (C) looked
   (D) searched

4. Fear of spiders is once of the most common types of phobias.
        (A)   (B) (C)   (D)

PART 2 RELATED ARTICLE

最初の解説で，クモには7つの目的別腺がある，と書きましたが，「一種のクモ」で，7つのすべてをもつものは，これまでのところ一つも見つかっていません。それではここで，アメリカ産の猛毒グモ「クロゴケグモ」(black widow) にかまれた時の治療法を記しておきましょう。▷かまれた箇所を石けん水でよく洗う　▷傷口を氷で冷やす　▷抗生物質入りクリーム (antibiotic cream) もしくはローションを塗布し，感染症 (infection) を防ぐ　▷痛みがある時はアセトアミノフェン (acetaminophen) を服用する。　▷これ以上の治療は病院で至急うける。時には，蛇毒血清 (antivenin) による対処・入院の必要が出てくる　▷子供の場合は特に，合併症 (complications) にならないように，すばやい手当が必要。下にあげる英文は「ゴールデンコガネグモ」(golden orb weaver) に関する解説です。空所に入る適当な動詞を，ⓐ～ⓔの中から1つずつ選び，入れてみてください。

Golden Orb Weaver (Argiope aurantia)

　　Females (¹　　　　) from 19 to 28 mm across (3/4 to 11/8 inches), while males (²　　　　) only 5 to 9 mm (1/4 - 3/8 inches).

　　In both sexes, the shiny, egg-shaped abdomen (³　　　　) striking yellow or orange markings on a black background. The forward part of the body, the cephalothorax, (⁴　　　　) covered with short, silvery hairs. Legs are mostly black, with red or yellow portions near the body. Like other orb-weavers, this spider has three claws per foot, one more than most spiders. Orb-weavers (⁵　　　　) this third claw to help handle the threads while spinning.

ⓐ range　ⓑ is　ⓒ reach　ⓓ has　ⓔ use

【語句】In both sexes「オス，メスとも」, abdomen「腹部」, striking「あざやかな」, cephalothorax「頭胸部」, claws「ツメ」

For Your Information

日本には約1300種類のクモが，世界中には約3万5000種のクモがいる。網を張らないクモの数が，張るものより，多い。セアカゴケグモ (redback spider) のような，毒液を出すクモもある。

16. Europa's Icy Sea

エウロペの氷の海

PART 1 SCIENCE TOPICS

1610年，ガリレオが発見した木星の2番目の衛星 (the second of the Galilean moons)，それが「エウロペ」です。木星には，16個以上の衛星 (satellites) があることが知られており，その中で4番目の大きさで，月よりちょっと小さいのがエウロペです。ギリシャ神話では，エウロペはフェニキア王の娘 (Phoenician princess) で，彼女に恋したゼウス (Zeus) は白い雄牛に姿を変え，彼女を誘拐し背に乗せてクレタ島に渡り結ばれた，と伝えられています。エウロペがこのときめぐり歩いた地方が，「ヨーロッパ」といわれるようになったといいます。また，エウロペとゼウスの間に産まれたのがクレタ島の王「ミノス」(Minos) です。木星の第2衛星の名前の由来を知った今，この衛星がいっそうロマンに輝く存在に思えてきませんか？

VOCABULARY

▶ Write the English words that correspond to following Japanese.

1. 卵　殻（らんかく）　→e _____
2. 亀　裂（きれつ）　→c _____
3. 引　力　　　　　　→g _____
4. 張　力（ちょうりょく）→sq _____
5. 測　量　　　　　　→m _____

LISTENING

▶ Listen to the tape, and mark your answers.

• Questions 1 through 4 refer to the following report.

1. How did astronomers learn that there might be water on Europa?

   (A) Jupiter reported the results of its research.
   (B) We could see it with the Hubble telescope.
   (C) Voyager radioed back photographs of the surface ice.
   (D) The tides caused by the moon were larger on Jupiter than expected.　Ⓐ Ⓑ Ⓒ Ⓓ

2. How was Europa different than expected?

   (A) It was very cold.
   (B) It was covered with ice.
   (C) It was closer to Jupiter than expected.
   (D) It didn't have many meteor craters.　Ⓐ Ⓑ Ⓒ Ⓓ

3. What is the cause of the cracks in the surface?

   (A) Meteor strikes.
   (B) The Moon's gravity.
   (C) The Voyager spacecraft.
   (D) Water pulled by gravity.　　　　　　　　　　　Ⓐ Ⓑ Ⓒ Ⓓ

4. Why does Europa have such massive sea tides?

   (A) Because Jupiter's gravity is very strong.
   (B) Because it is far away from the Sun's heat.
   (C) Because the sea is covered with a thick layer of ice.
   (D) Because there is no one there to measure the temperature.　　Ⓐ Ⓑ Ⓒ Ⓓ

Check it out!

　今，皆さんが取り組んだ Part Ⅳ の問題は，174語構成でこのパートの基準でも最も長い部類に入ります。この長さの「説明文問題」に出くわすのは，TOEIC®テストを連続5回受験して1度くらい，とお考え下さい。つまり，この長さのリスニング問題の出題例は最近では少なく，ただし，出題された時は必ず「関連問題4題」となることは十分ご理解下さい。上の問題の「長さ」に触れ，「感触」を知り，免疫をつくることはとても重要といえます。戦略としては，テストブックに印刷されている関連問題の「事前読みによる音声内容予測」がとてもとても大切なことだと実感できたのではないでしょうか。

READING

▶ Look at the following chart and answer the questions after it. Questions #1 and #2 test your comprehension. In Question #3, choose the answer that best completes the sentence. In Question #4, find the error in the sentence.

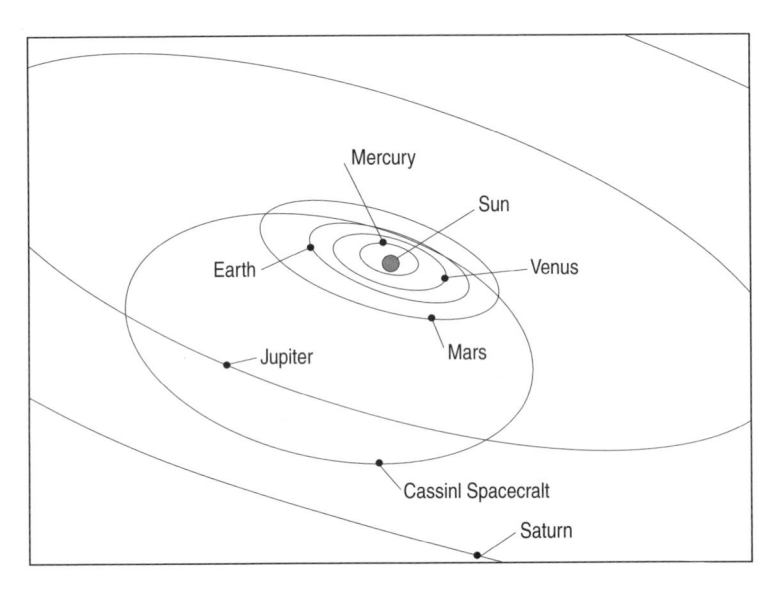

The Cassini Mission to Study Jupiter and Saturn

1. What kind of information does this graphic present?

   (A) Variation in the orbits of the planets affected by the mission.
   (B) The path of the Cassini spaceship during the course of its mission.
   (C) The course of the design and development of the Cassini spacecraft.
   (D) The position of our solar system in the universe during the mission.   Ⓐ Ⓑ Ⓒ Ⓓ

2. Where does the spacecraft reach the furthest point of its orbit from the sun?

   (A) Inside the orbit of the Earth.
   (B) Far outside of the path of Saturn.
   (C) Almost to the limits of Jupiter's orbit.
   (D) Between the orbits of Jupiter and Saturn.   Ⓐ Ⓑ Ⓒ Ⓓ

3. Unmanned space probes have greatly increased our _____ of our solar system.

   (A) seen   (B) visit   (C) understood   (D) knowledge   Ⓐ Ⓑ Ⓒ Ⓓ

4. <u>There</u> is some controversy <u>over</u> <u>which</u> Pluto is a small planet <u>or</u> a big asteroid.
     (A)   (B) (C)   (D)

   Ⓐ Ⓑ Ⓒ Ⓓ

PART 2 RELATED ARTICLE

木星（Jupiter）は太陽系の内側から５番目の惑星（the fifth planet）で，太陽系の惑星の中でも特別の大きさを誇り，その質量（mass）は他の太陽系惑星をすべて合計した２倍以上，地球の実に３１８倍もあります。宇宙探査機パイオニア１０号が，木星を初めて調査したのが１９７３年で，以後，パイオニア１１号・ボイジャー１号/２号・ユリシーズ号，が木星調査を行っています。現在，探査機ガリレオ号が木星軌道を周回中で（in orbit），少なくともあと数年は地球にデータ送信してくる予定です。木星は，９割の水素（hydrogen）と１割のヘリウム（helium）から主にできており，若干のメタン（methane）・水・アンモニア（ammonia）・岩石があることが判っています。この物質構成は，太陽系全体が誕生した「原始の太陽系星雲」（primordial Solar Nebula）と極めて似たものと宇宙天文学者たちは考えています。それでは問題です。下にあげた，イタリアの物理学者で天文学者の「ガリレオ・ガリレイ」の解説を読み，下線部の単語の品詞を変換し，文法的に正しい文にしてみて下さい。

Galileo Galilei (1564 - 1642)

Galileo Galilei was ① birth February 15, 1564 in Pisa. He studied medicine before switching to mathematics and science. In 1609, he learned of the ② invent of the telescope. He made his own telescope with a power of 40 times and had soon made dozens of discoveries about the solar system. He ③ discover the moons of Jupiter in 1610. ④ Him discoveries challenged the Catholic Church. The church claimed the earth ⑤ is the center of the universe. Galileo was arrested and forced to retract his views. His book ⑥ explain his ideas, 'Discourses on Two New Sciences,' was ⑦ final smuggled out of Italy and published in Netherlands in 1638.

① → _____   ② → _____   ③ → _____

④ → _____   ⑤ → _____   ⑥ → _____

⑦ → _____

For Your Information

木星は天空で，太陽・月・金星につぐ，４番目に明るい天体。また，ローマ神話では，「ユピテル」（Jupiter）と呼ばれる神々の王で，オリュンポス山の支配者・古代ローマの守護聖人でもあった。

17. Microbots

マイクロボット

PART 1 SCIENCE TOPICS

微細な可動装置を製造することを,「超微細加工技術」(micromachining) と呼び,遺伝子工学 (genetic engineering) 以来の最重要最先端技術の一つといわれています。すでに技術専門家たちは,ピンの頭よりも小さいモーター・1個の赤血球をつかまえられる装置・超微細歯車装置 (gear train)・超微細蒸気機関車などの製作に成功しています。現在,超微細装置の製作には,標準半導体技術 (standard semiconductor processes) が活かされています。超微細技術の商業化にいち早く成功した例に,「動くシリコン基板」(silicon that moves) や,「自動圧力センサー」(automative pressure sensors) があります。単純な圧力センサーが,シリコンウェファーから作られたのが1980年代初期で,同センサーで最初に商業的に大成功したのが,自動車のエアバッグ (automobile airbags) を作動させる「超微細衝突センサー」(micromechanical crash sensors) です。

VOCABULARY

▶ Match the items in the two columns.

1. overhead   ・   ・ a. high above one's head
2. clap   ・   ・ b. enterprise
3. tiny   ・   ・ c. keep for future use
4. project   ・   ・ d. small
5. store   ・   ・ e. applaud

LISTENING

▶ Listen to the tape, and mark your answers.

1.   Ⓐ Ⓑ Ⓒ Ⓓ

2.   Ⓐ Ⓑ Ⓒ Ⓓ

3. Ⓐ Ⓑ Ⓒ Ⓓ

4. Ⓐ Ⓑ Ⓒ Ⓓ

5. Ⓐ Ⓑ Ⓒ Ⓓ

6. Ⓐ Ⓑ Ⓒ Ⓓ

─ *Check it out !* ─

　PartⅠの音声選択肢の正解の8割は「現在進行形」で，残りの2割は「現在形」です。つまり，「…です」という意味で，具体的には、The sidewalk is slippery because of the rain.「雨で歩道はすべりやすくなっています」/ The woman is dressed for cold weather.「女性は防寒用の服装をしています」といった形を指します。また，このパートで読まれる選択肢短文は，平均して，8語構成だということも理解しておきましょう。The men seem to be in a hurry.「男性たちは急いでいるようです」（8語構成）。そして，これが，2秒で読まれますので，スピードに慣れるようにしましょう。

READING

▶ Read the following passage and answer the questions after it. Questions #1 and #2 test your comprehension. In Question #3, choose the answer that best completes the sentence. In Question #4, find the error in the sentence.

Robots have replaced humans in many jobs. They are strong, they do very precise work and they don't take lunch breaks or vacations. These days, as electronics have become smaller and more powerful, robots are shrinking too. Some are based on the study of insects. These "bugbots" are designed to do simple jobs. Using sensors and a few basic commands, they can crawl into areas that are too dangerous or too small for humans, such as collapsed buildings, sewer lines or minefields. Now scientists are learning to make even smaller robots. Microbots, or microelectromechanical systems (MEMS), are made using the same techniques that build computer chips. By combining tiny gears, drive chains and levers, microscopic machines can be made. Experts expect thousands of uses for the microbots as the technology improves and they become even smaller and more complex. They may even become small enough to inject inside humans for microscopic medical therapy. They will be repairing humans instead of replacing them.

1. Why are robots better than humans for some jobs?
   (A) They can think independently.
   (B) Humans don't like insects very much.
   (C) They work more carefully than humans.
   (D) They have to take vacations more often for work.

2. How has computer chip manufacturing lead to smaller microbots?
   (A) The same methods are used to make them.
   (B) Computer engineers are impressed in making robots.
   (C) Computer workstations are perfect for building them.
   (D) They have the same types of "bugs" as computer chips.

3. Many simple machines are often more efficient than a _____ complex one.
   (A) but   (B) only   (C) single   (D) primary

4. Insects are <u>capable</u> of complex <u>behaving</u>, <u>despite</u> their <u>simple</u> brains.
                (A)   (B)   (C)   (D)

PART 2 RELATED ARTICLE

ここで，米企業・大学が「超微細技術」をどう応用し，ビジネスに結びつけようとしているか，みてみましょう。　▷ゼロックス社のＰＡＲＣ工場では，プリンタのグレードアップに，超微細バルブ/エアジェットを開発中　▷ＵＣＬＡ大学の科学者グループは，より精度の高いかじ取りに必要な，飛行機の翼（つばさ）に装備する「超微細フラップ」を研究中　▷ウィスコンシン大学の研究者グループは，強度のＸ線平板印刷（lithography）と電解折出（electrodeposition）を用いた，超微細ギヤ/モーターを製作中　▷ルーセント・テクノロジー社の科学者グループは，広帯域光ファイバーケーブル（high-bandwidth fiber optic cable）を通るぼう大な光の量を制御するのに超微細技術（MEMS）利用を検討中

それではここで，ＭＥＭＳ関連の英文を読み，設問に答えてみて下さい。

Many of these astounding MEMS devices have yet to escape the laboratory, although just as
　　　　　　　　　　　　　　　　　　　　　①

many continue to go into the commercial marketplace, becoming more and more a part of
②　　　　　　　　　　　　　　　　　　　　　　　　　　　③

our electronic daily lives.

1. ①の意味を下の ⓐ～ⓒ のどれが正解でしょうか。
   ⓐ 実験室からようやく脱出した
   ⓑ やっと実験室で研究が始まった
   ⓒ いぜんとして実験室での研究段階にある

2. manyの後に省略されている語句は何でしょうか。

3. 現在分詞 'becoming' が修飾する単語は何でしょうか。

For Your Information

　全米で，ナノテクノロジー（nanotechnology）と MEMS を平行しながら，大がかりな研究開発プログラムを進めている。注目度 No.1 はコーネル大学の「ナノファブリケーション研究所」（Nanofabrication Facility）だ。年間350万ドルの連邦政府補助をうけ，3000万ドルの研究設備を誇る。

18. Alien Hitchhikers

宇宙からのヒッチハイカー

PART 1 SCIENCE TOPICS

アイオワ州立大学の微生物学 (microbiology) の準教授，デニス・バズィリンスキィ氏の研究チームは，火星 (Mars) にかつて原始生命体 (primitive life) がいた，という驚くべき証拠をみつけました。火星からきた隕石 (Martian meteorite) の中に，磁場に反応して生物が示す，磁気走性バクテリア (magnetotactic bacteria) による独特の運動が認められたのです。1984年，南極で発見された，45億年前に降ってきた隕石の磁鉄鉱結晶 (magnetite crystals) から，この事実を突きとめたのです。磁気走性バクテリアが作る磁鉄鉱結晶は，化学的に純粋で，しかも大きさと形状に特徴があります。

結局，研究チームは，隕石の磁鉄鉱結晶の約4分の1が，'MV-1' と呼ばれるバクテリアが作ったものと結論を下しました。宇宙生物学 (astrobiology) と地球生物学 (geobiology) にとって重要なことは，生命の存在根拠を示す「バイオマーカー」(biomarkers) が特定できれば，宇宙物質・地上の古代物質・極限の生息地にかかわらず，生命体をさぐる手がかりとなることです。

VOCABULARY

▶ Choose the word that has the same meaning as the underlined one.

1. What are the <u>chances</u> of your business succeeding?
   a. probability   b. happening   c. event

2. The company <u>announced</u> a drive for cost containment.
   a. occurred   b. held   c. made known

3. The introduction of <u>protective</u> masks is not what we're negotiating this time.
   a. relating   b. intended to protect   c. wearing

LISTENING

▶ **Listen to the tape, and mark your answers.**

1. Mark your answer on your answer sheet.   Ⓐ Ⓑ Ⓒ

2. Mark your answer on your answer sheet.   Ⓐ Ⓑ Ⓒ

3. Mark your answer on your answer sheet.   Ⓐ Ⓑ Ⓒ

4. Mark your answer on your answer sheet.   Ⓐ Ⓑ Ⓒ

5. Mark your answer on your answer sheet.   Ⓐ Ⓑ Ⓒ

6. Mark your answer on your answer sheet.   Ⓐ Ⓑ Ⓒ

7. Mark your answer on your answer sheet.   Ⓐ Ⓑ Ⓒ

Check it out!

　PartⅡの質問の「残り25％」を占めるのが，「付加疑問文/否定疑問文/選択疑問文」です。
　<付加疑問文>「…ですよね？/…でないですよね？」と，相手に「確認」をとったり「念を押す」時に用いられます。Q: Kim has been transferred to Portugal, hasn't he?「キムはリスボンへ転勤になったんですよね？」→正解の選択肢：Yes, to Lisbon.
　<否定疑問文>「…じゃないの？」と相手にたずねる疑問文。Q: Isn't this high-speed wireless network revolutionary?「この高速ワイヤレス・ネットワークって，革命的じゃないの？」→正解の選択肢：You got that right.「本当，革命的だよ」
　<選択疑問文>「XとYのどっちかしら？」と相手にたずねる疑問文。Q: Which is more cost saving, temp staffing or contract staffing?「どっちが経費の節約になる？派遣によるスタッフ補充，それとも契約社員によるスタッフ補充？」→正解の選択肢: Contract staffing, if you ask me.「契約社員によるスタッフ補充だと，ボクは思うけど」
　いかがですか？上にあげた「3つの疑問文」にも慣れておくようにしましょう。

Alien Hitchhikers

READING

▶ Read the following passage and answer the questions after it. Questions #1 and #2 test your comprehension. In Question #3, choose the answer that best completes the sentence. In Question #4, find the error in the sentence.

Scientists have always thought that nothing could live in outer space. It is cold and dry, and there is no air. Now they aren't so sure. In 1996, NASA announced that its scientists might have found fossils of alien bacteria on a meteorite from Mars. The fossils were chains of magnetite crystals. They were similar to the crystals found in some earth bacteria. The fossils show that bacteria could possibly hitchhike through space on rocks. The problem would be surviving the many years in space and the fiery landing on Earth. But bacteria are turning out to be a lot tougher than we thought. They have been found almost everywhere on earth, no matter how hot, cold, dry or radioactive it is. Many of them can go into a protective sleep for thousands, or even millions, of years. When conditions are better, they wake up. If the fossils are really from bacteria, then that could be where life on earth began, on another planet. Our ancestors could be space aliens.

1. What fossil evidence did NASA find of alien bacteria?
    (A) Living bacteria.
    (B) Bacterial bones.
    (C) Metallic crystals.
    (D) DNA chemicals.   Ⓐ Ⓑ Ⓒ Ⓓ

2. Where were the fossils found?
    (A) On rocks from the moon.
    (B) On a rock that fell to the Earth.
    (C) On the surface of the planet Mars.
    (D) On a meteorite traveling through space.   Ⓐ Ⓑ Ⓒ Ⓓ

3. The Amazon rain forest is one _____ the most diverse ecosystems on earth.
    (A) to (B) of (C) by (D) for   Ⓐ Ⓑ Ⓒ Ⓓ

4. <u>Boil</u> for twenty minutes in water <u>will</u> kill <u>even</u> the <u>hardiest</u> bacteria.   Ⓐ Ⓑ Ⓒ Ⓓ
    (A)   (B)   (C)   (D)

PART 2 RELATED ARTICLE

米国の自治領プエルトリコの北部にある港湾都市アレシボに，アレシボ観測所（Arecibo Observatory）があります。ここでは毎日，電波望遠鏡（radio telescope）を用い，宇宙にいるかもしれない文明人から発せられる電波信号を傍受する作業を行っています。楽しいですが，難しい作業でもあり，分析を要するデータが山ほどあります。ただ，幸いなことに，データ分析作業（data analysis task）は簡単に分割し，分担できるとのことです。そして，実は，あなたも，アレシボ観測所の呼びかける「あなたの自宅から参加できるデータ分析計画」（SETI@home）に協力できます。<http://www.setiathome.ssl.berkeley.edu/>
それではここで，「SETI@home計画」への参加を呼びかける英文を抜粋してみますから，設問に答えてみて下さい。

This is where SETI@home (and you!) come into the picture. The SETI@home project hopes
　　　　　　　　　　　①　　　　　　　　　　　　　　　　　　　　　　　　　　　　　②
to convince you to allow us to borrow your computer when you aren't using it and to help us
　　③
"search out new life and new civilizations."

① この一文の意味は？ ⓐ～ⓒ の中から正解を選びましょう。
　　ⓐ このホームページで，SETI@home と一緒に，あなたも宇宙の写真が楽しめる。
　　ⓑ そこで，SETI@home 計画とあなたの協力が必要になってくるわけです。
　　ⓒ ここをクリックすると，SETI@home とあなたは，協力しながら宇宙写真を撮影することができます。
② この同意語を ⓐ～ⓒ から1つ選びましょう。
　　ⓐ proposal　ⓑ enterprise　ⓒ propaganda
③ この反意語を ⓐ～ⓒ から1つ選びましょう。
　　ⓐ dissuade　ⓑ concern　ⓒ convert
④ 'it' とは何のこと？

For Your Information

　'SETI@home' 計画へ，自分のパソコンを使い，ネットを経由し協力してみるのも「生きた学習」といえるだろう。ありとあらゆる天文学のトピックを取り扱っているホームページに 'Astronomy Interactive Network <http://www.library.thinkquest.org/15418/home.html> がある。

19. Land Mines

地雷

PART 1 SCIENCE TOPICS

▷地雷敷設（ふせつ）総数 → 世界64カ国に1億1000万
▷地雷による死傷者数 → 月平均800人の死者。犠牲者の大部分は民間人で，生涯肢体不自由者(those maimed for life)の数は毎月数千人にのぼる
▷地雷購入費・撤去費 → 地雷1つの値段：3～10ドル。地雷1つの撤去費：300～1000ドル

…地雷は古代中国で発明されました。国連人道問題課(United Nations Department of Humanitarian Affairs)の資料によると、「地雷敷設数の多い国のベスト3」は、エジプト<2300万> / イラン<1600万> / アンゴラ<1500万>。「1平方マイルあたりの地雷数の多い国ベスト3」は、ボスニア・ヘルツェゴビナ<152> / カンボジア<143> / クロアチア<137>，となっています。

VOCABULARY

▶ Write the English words that correspond to following Japanese words.

1. スケジュール →s_____　2. ロビー →l_____
3. 爆　弾 →b_____　4. 放火魔 →ar_____
5. 外科医 →s_____

LISTENING

▶ Listen to the tape, and mark your answers.

1. What does the woman think will happen?

　(A) She doesn't know.
　(B) They will miss their next flight.
　(C) They will catch their next flight.
　(D) Their next flight will be delayed.　　Ⓐ Ⓑ Ⓒ Ⓓ

2. What did the woman see happening in the lobby this morning?

　(A) A bond sale.
　(B) A dog show.
　(C) A home show.
　(D) A bomb search.　　Ⓐ Ⓑ Ⓒ Ⓓ

3. How did the fire begin?

   (A) It was started by a stray cigarette.
   (B) It was set on purpose by someone.
   (C) It was set off by an electronic machine.
   (D) Car exhaust accidentally started the fire.

4. What kind of danger has been prevented in the surrounding area?

   (A) Wooden trees.
   (B) Hungry bears.
   (C) Angry cleaners.
   (D) Buried explosives.

5. What did the men just see?

   (A) An exploding oil tanker.
   (B) A fire in a skyscraper.
   (C) The demolition of a building.
   (D) The construction of a gambling casino.

Check it out !

　PartⅢのテストブックに印刷されている疑問詞 Who / How の,「音声の聞きどころ」について追加しておきましょう。▷Who<音声対話中の「人物」に注意して聴く>　▷How <「手段：方法」に注意しながら対話を聴く>…となります。このパートのスコアを切り上げるには、これまで述べた「戦略」と平行して、交わされる「対話をイメージ化」するスキルが大切です。

　　（例）　　W：Are there any downsides to success?
　　　　　　　M: Yes, a few. The big winners must have the generosity to step aside.
　　　　　　　W: You mean, you have to show a willingness to compromise?

<イメージ>W：成功のマイナス面は？→M：少しだけ。弱者にゆずる度量が求められる→W：妥協せざるをえないところが出てくるってこと？
<戦略> 女性記者が業績絶好調のトップにインタビューしている場面を「画像」として残す練習をくり返してみましょう。

Land Mines

READING

▶ Read the following passage and answer the questions after it. Questions #1 and #2 test your comprehension. In Question #3, choose the answer that best completes the sentence. In Question #4, find the error in the sentence.

The most common tool in the world for detecting land mines is a stick. Someone has to crawl on the ground poking gently at the dirt until they find a mine. It's not a very popular job. High-tech machines that can find mines are available, but they are expensive. It is usually the poorest countries where mines are used. They cost as little as $3 apiece. What is needed is a cheap, portable, effective detector to find the mines. Several such detectors are being developed. One, called a Timed Neutron Detector, detects the hydrogen in the mine's case or explosives. Another detects the mine's explosive fumes. It sets off microexplosions when the fumes touch a tiny heated wire. That tells the detector that a mine is nearby. Soon, detectors, the size of a flashlight, could be selling for as little as $300. At that price, any country can afford them.

1. What is the most widely used method for detecting buried mines?
   (A) Manual probing.
   (B) Metal detectors.
   (C) Satellite photography.
   (D) Timed neutron detectors.

2. Why are land mines most often used in poor countries?
   (A) Because they are very dangerous.
   (B) Because poor countries have more enemies.
   (C) Because rich countries don't often go to war.
   (D) Because they are one of the cheapest weapons.

3. The effects of war often _____ for many years after the fighting ends.
   (A) last   (B) more   (C) cause   (D) forgot

4. Over the last few centuries, civilians have became the primary targets of war.
     (A)   (B)   (C)   (D)

PART 2 RELATED ARTICLE

地雷には２種類あります。「対戦車用地雷」(anti-tank mine:AT) と「対人用地雷」(anti-personnel mine: AP) です。地雷は，通常，人のクツより大きく，重さは５キロ以上あります。爆発による殺傷能力は，この上を走る車輌を破壊し，車輌内もしくは近くにいる人を殺すほどです。この対戦車用地雷は，敵側の車・トラックが走行すると思われる道路・橋・輸送路などに敷設されます。これに対し，対人用地雷は軽量小型で，中にはタバコの箱サイズで重さがわずか50グラムのものもあり，兵士を負傷させるのが目的です。それではここで，問題です。下にあげる対人用地雷に関する英文記事を読み，空所に入る適切な前置詞をⓐ～ⓔの中から１つ選び，入れてみて下さい。

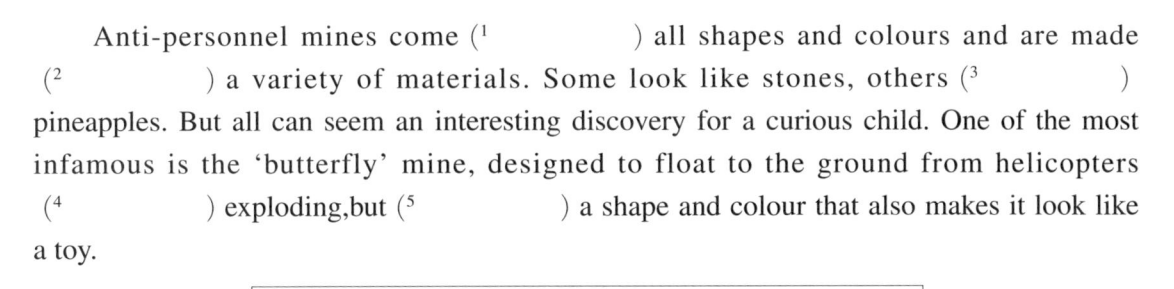

Anti-personnel mines come (¹   ) all shapes and colours and are made (²   ) a variety of materials. Some look like stones, others (³   ) pineapples. But all can seem an interesting discovery for a curious child. One of the most infamous is the 'butterfly' mine, designed to float to the ground from helicopters (⁴   ) exploding, but (⁵   ) a shape and colour that also makes it look like a toy.

ⓐ in   ⓑ without   ⓒ with   ⓓ from   ⓔ like

【語句】Some = Some anti-personnel mines。others = other anti-personnel minesで，この後の 'look' の省略に注意。all = all anti-personnel mines。one of the most infamous (anti-personnel mines)「最も悪名高い対人用地雷の１つ」の（   ）内の省略にも注意。ネイティブの書く英文は「ともかく省略が多い」ことに注意しよう。彼らは，「分かりきっていることは明示する必要がない」と考えるのが原則です。   it = the butterfly mine。

For Your Information

人名に由来する兵器は多い。Kalashnikov「AK−47：自動小銃」（開発者名）/ Sikorski「シコルスキー型ヘリコプター」（開発技術者名）/ shrapnel「りゅう散弾」（発明者名）/ Big Bertha「大砲」（ドイツの鉄工場社長名）/ Winchester「ウィンチェスター連発銃」（製造者名）/ Colt「コルト銃」（発明者名）… などがある。

20. Child Prodigy

神童

PART 1 SCIENCE TOPICS

知能テスト（intelligence quotient tests: IQ tests）はどんな経緯で開発されたのでしょうか？フランス政府は，能力があってもヤル気のない生徒と，能力不足の生徒を住み分けるテストはできないものかと思案し，アルフレッド・ビネーを任命し，開発に着手しました。そして，心理学者ビネーは1905年に，世界最初の個別用知能検査を創案したのです。

1920年代に入ると，スタンフォード大学教授のルイス・ターマンが米国版知能テストを開発し，カリフォルニア州立学校の数百名の生徒を対象に行いましたが，同テストは「スタンフォード・ビネー知能テスト」（Stanford-Binet test）として知られています。当時の知能テストは，年齢別で，平均的な能力の子供に比べて，ある子供がどれ位，上か下か，を判断する方式でした。でも，今日のIQテストは，過去60年間のテストデータを基に作成した標準偏差値をベースにしスコアを決めるやり方で，もはや「比率」（quotient）とは言えません。

VOCABULARY

▶ Match the items in the two columns.

1. gifted   ・   ・ a. demanding
2. challenging   ・   ・ b. lack of success
3. restroom   ・   ・ c. toilet
4. prodigy   ・   ・ d. young person with exceptional abilities
5. failure   ・   ・ d. having a natural ability

LISTENING

▶ Listen to the tape, and mark your answers.

Questions 1 and 2 refer to the following talk.

1. Who would be the audience for this speech?

    (A) Students.

    (B) Mothers and Fathers.

    (C) Local businessmen.

    (D) School administrators.   Ⓐ Ⓑ Ⓒ Ⓓ

2. How is this program different from a regular high school education?

    (A) It is the same.

    (B) It focuses more on the arts.

    (C) It is easier than the regular classes.

    (D) It is more difficult than other classes. Ⓐ Ⓑ Ⓒ Ⓓ

84

Questions 3 and 4 refer to the following announcement.

3. When will the test begin?

   (A) Very soon.
   (B) Immediately.
   (C) After the study period is over.
   (D) After the teacher goes to the bathroom. Ⓐ Ⓑ Ⓒ Ⓓ

4. What are students permitted to have on their desk, besides pencils?

   (A) A calculator.
   (B) Study materials.
   (C) A mobile telephone.
   (D) An electronic pager. Ⓐ Ⓑ Ⓒ Ⓓ

Check it out !

　Part Ⅳのスコアを切り上げ，実社会で使える「リスニング力」を身につけるには，何といっても「情報のイメージ化」のスキルがものを言います。相手の発言を「単語単位」としてでなく，「情報単位」として頭の中に残す技術を「例」でしめしますので、見てみましょう。

<例>　音声：Supplying cheap labor is only the first step on the economic development structure. Such jobs are never permanent in growth economies, but some management people have ignored this fact and their futures. Their goals should be this; providing sophisticated products and services to world markets.

情報単位：低賃金労働力の働く場所を提供するのは，経済発展の第1段階だ。この発想が高成長経済国では通用しない。経営者の中には，この事実に目をつむり，未来展望という視点のない者もいる。経営目標はあくまでも，高性能製品とサービス業務を世界の市場に売りこむことにつきる。

イメージ化：場所 / 経営セミナー会場。講演者 / 経営コンサルタント。演壇に立ったスミス氏は口を開いていう。いいかな，「低賃金の労働市場とは経済発展の一番下のレベルじゃ。低賃金の職場は高成長経済国になれば，やがてなくなる。だがじゃ，勘違いしとるトップもいるのう。目先の利益ばかり追いかけて，将来の展望ちゅうものがない。付加価値の高い商品とサービスを，世界を相手にバンバン売ることだ」

戦略：これ位，オーバーに，ある「人」や「物」を想定し，情報をつみ上げくっつけていくと，「話の内容が記憶に残る確率」がかなりアップします。いろんな素材を用い，練習してみましょう。

READING

▶ Read the following passage and answer the questions after it. Questions #1 and #2 test your comprehension. In Question #3, choose the answer that best completes the sentence. In Question #4, find the error in the sentence.

Being A Genius The Key To Success?

It's not easy being a genius, especially when you are young. Many people are envious of child prodigies. The kid has it made, they think. Sometimes it's true. Mozart was writing symphonies by the time he was eight and he became one of the greatest composers in history. But sometimes the pressure is too much. William Sidis was a famous child prodigy from the early 1900's. At two years of age, he was already reading the New York Times. By the time he was eight, he could speak six languages and had written four books. He entered Harvard University at age eleven. Newspaper reporters followed him everywhere, expecting him to become a great man. But they happily reported his failures, too. When he died at forty-four, after a life of simple, low-paying jobs, he was an angry and lonely man. Many child prodigies go on to become average people and many very successful people were average children. It seems that success in life takes more than a high I.Q.

1. What is a prodigy?

    (A) Someone who is older than most children.
    (B) A person who can speak many languages.
    (C) A child who is very advanced for his age.
    (D) Someone whose IQ is not as high as average.

2. Why was William Sidis considered a failure by the public?

    (A) He never graduated from university.
    (B) He couldn't speak English very well.
    (C) He never learned to read the books he wrote.
    (D) He didn't become as successful as expected.

3. Even children _____ develop at different rates usually end up as normal adults.

    (A) but   (B) who   (C) then   (D) what

4. Emotional development doesn't always goes at the same pace as intelligence.
                                   (A)   (B) (C)   (D)

PART 2 RELATED ARTICLE

「知性とは知能テストの測定結果のすべて」といったスターンバーグ氏は，1985年に，知能テストの特徴を3つあげています。知識の量 / 世界・世間の出来事を推論する能力 / 場面によって推論を調整できる能力の3つです。今日よく用いられる知能テストの1つに，米国の心理学者ディヴィッド・ウェクスラーが開発した，客観的標準偏差値（objective, standardized scale）を用いたテストがあります。ウェクスラー式成人知能テスト / ウェクスラー式児童知能テスト / ウェクスラー・ベルビュー知能テスト，などがあり，「言語能力テスト」（verbal scale）・「年齢比較総合能力テスト」（scores reflect relative standing with/in a population of your age）・「動作性能力テスト」（performance scale）の3種類があり，知的能力を要素別に詳しく調べるのが特徴といえます。それではここで問題です。次の英文を読み設問に答えてみて下さい。

Henry Goddard adapted① Binet's test for use② with U.S. Immigration. His intelligence tests were biased③ and unfair, requiring familiarity④ with American culture. The test was later the basis for the Army Alpha & Beta tests that were mainly used during World War I⑤ to deploy newly recruited soldiers.

① この単語の同意語は次のうちどれ？
　　ⓐ make do　ⓑ make good　ⓒ make suitable
② この単語の品詞は？
③ この単語の意味は？
　　ⓐ 偏向した　ⓑ 変身した　ⓒ 変幻自在の
④ このコンテキストでのこの単語の意味は？
　　ⓐ 知識　ⓑ 顔なじみ　ⓒ 親交
⑤ この語句はどう読む？

For Your Information

　IQテストの最高レベルは，149ポイント以上で，この範ちゅうに入る人は全体の0.13％しかいない。現在生存する人物の中で，最もIQが高いといわれている人は'Parade Magazine'に，＜なんでもマリリンにきいてみな＞というコラムを持つ女性，マリリン・フォス・サヴァン（Marilyn vos Savant）。なんと，彼女は1989年度版のギネス・ブックで最高のIQの持ち主と紹介された。そのスコアは…228。

本書にはカセットテープ(別売)があります

Cutting Edge in Science
―サイエンストピックで学ぶ英語―

2005年3月20日　新装版発行
2011年2月20日　重版発行

　　　著　者　　　松　野　守　峰
　　　　　　　　　Ruskyle L. Howser
　　　発行者　　　福　岡　靖　雄
　　　発行所　　　株式会社　金　星　堂
　　　(〒101-0051) 東京都千代田区神田神保町 3-21
　　　　　　　　Tel. (03) 3263-3828 (営業部)
　　　　　　　　　　(03) 3263-3997 (編集部)
　　　　　　　　Fax (03) 3263-0716
　　　　　　　　http://www.kinsei-do.co.jp

印刷所／加藤文明社　製本所／松島製本　　　1-23-3768
落丁・乱丁本はお取り替えいたします

ISBN978-4-7647-3768-6　C1082